Structuralism

An Interdisciplinary Study

edited by
Susan Wittig

The Pickwick Press
Pittsburgh, Pennsylvania
1975

Originally published by SOUNDINGS, an Interdisciplinary Journal, Vol. LVIII, No. 2, Summer 1975. Grateful acknowledgement to the former editor of SOUNDINGS, Sallie TeSelle, for the arrangements made for this special issue.

Library of Congress Cataloging in Publication Data
Main entry under title:

Structuralism : an interdisciplinary study.

(Pittsburgh reprint series ; 3)
"Originally published by Soundings, an interdisciplinary journal, vol. LVIII, no. 2, Summer 1975."
Includes bibliographies.
1. Structuralism (Literary analysis) 2. Folklore--Structural analysis. I. Wittig, Susan. II. Soundings (Nashville)
PN98.S7S8 809 76-899
ISBN 0-915138-16-6

THE PICKWICK PRESS
5001 BAUM BLVD.
PITTSBURGH, PA. 15213

PITTSBURGH REPRINT SERIES

General Editor
Dikran Y. Hadidian

3

STRUCTURALISM

An Interdisciplinary Study

CONTENTS

THE HISTORICAL DEVELOPMENT OF STRUCTURALISM

SUSAN WITTIG

THE WRITING OF A REVIEW of the historical development of structuralism seems to imply, among other things, that structuralism as a philosophic movement is a finished bit of business, a completed act in the drama of man's attempts to explain himself to himself—and (according to some critics) one that somehow never fulfilled its potential. Indeed, in their 1971 introduction to the re-edition of *The Structuralist Controversy*, Richard Macksey and Eugenio Donato point out that Foucault, Lacan, Derrida—among others whose names had early been associated with the structuralist movement—have felt obliged to "take their distance" from the term:

> Today we may question the very existence of structuralism as a meaningful concept, for not the last of the paradoxes generated by what has come to be known as the structuralist controversy is the fact that as an operative concept it is more evident in the language of its detractors and popularizers than in the express statements of those who are supposed to be its main proponents.[1]

Yet despite this disclaimer, and despite the frequent expressions of critical unease with the structuralist enterprise in its various manifestations, structural methodologies, theories, and philosophies have become a vital intellectual force in the work of

Dr. Wittig is an Assistant Professor at the University of Texas, Austin, where she teaches courses in medieval literature, comparative literature and literary theory. She is the translator of Boris Uspensky's *The Poetics of Composition*, and the author of several essays on semiotics. Her book, *Structural Studies of Middle English Verse Romances*, will be published by Mouton.

the current generation of students and scholars, who from the vantage point of the mid '70s can see the growth of a philosophical school from its beginnings in the linguistic study of the surface structures of language, through the description and analysis of formal features of literary works, through the study of generative patterns in human society, through psychology and history, through the varied studies of man, his culture, his artifacts. Although it is too early to write a definitive history of the structuralist movement, and certainly far too early to write *finis* to its development, it is surely time again to pause for its review and to contemplate the more recent contributions to the study of the humane sciences.

Structuralism has its methodological beginnings in the structural linguistics of Ferdinand de Saussure, whose synchronic study of language systems stands in sharp contrast to the diachronic and comparative studies of nineteenth-century philology. Saussure, whose lectures on general linguistics have been preserved in the notes and transcriptions of two of his students, Charles Bally and Charles Schehaye, taught at the University of Geneva from 1906 to 1911, where he formulated his theories of language.[2] His major concern was to reconstitute the science of linguistics as a *systematic* study which focuses on both the structural and the functional features of language. The basis of that systematic study, he believed, should be the synchronic analysis of the state of the language at any given point in time—the formal and functional description of the regularities and laws which govern speech. Linguistics must also engage, however, in *diachronic* study, he argued, in the examination of the dynamic forces which produce language evolution. To illustrate this idea he compared the study of language to the analysis of a game of chess. John Lyons has usefully summarized Saussure's analogy:

> In the course of a game of chess the state of the board is constantly changing, but at any one time the state of the game can be fully described in terms of the positions occupied by the several pieces. It does not matter by what route (the number, nature or order of the moves) the players have arrived at the particular state of the game: this state is describable *synchronically* without reference to the previous moves. So it is with language, said de Saussure. All languages are constantly changing; and just as the state of the chess-board at some particular time can be described without reference to the particular combination of moves that has brought the game to that point, so

> can the successive, or socially and geographically delimited, states of a language be described independently of one another.[3]

Saussure's suggestion that these two kinds of study, carefully distinguished and thoughtfully balanced so that the synchronic description complements and is complemented by the diachronic description, has had repercussions beyond the sciences of language, as he suggested it should:

> Certainly all sciences would profit by indicating more precisely the coordinates along which their subject matter is aligned . . . For a science concerned with values the distinction [between synchronic and diachronic study] is a practical necessity and sometimes an absolute one. In these fields scholars cannot organize their research rigorously without considering both coordinates and making a distinction between the system of values per se and the same values as they relate to time.[4]

Saussure's second major contribution to structuralist thought grows out of this same temporal/non-temporal dichotomy. He suggests that language acquires meaning along two axes of relationships: the *syntagmatic* or linear-temporal axis of unfolding speech, occurring in time; and the *paradigmatic* axis—non-linear, non-temporally ordered—of associative meaning.[5] On the syntagmatic axis (the "axis of successions") signs have meaning by virtue of their opposition to the sign that precedes and the sign that follows in the syntactical chain: we can make sense of the morpheme "pin," for instance, because we can distinguish the three phonemes p/i/n; we can make sense of the words on this page because each can be distinguished from the word ahead of it and the word behind it. The syntagm is the combination of the opposing or contrasting signs, united *in praesentia* in the moment of speech. On the paradigmatic axis (the "axis of simultaneity"), however, a sign has meaning by virtue of the fact that it enters into associative relations with all of the signs that might occur in the same syntagmatic context with it (that is, with a group of signs which are all structurally homologous). Therefore we can make sense of the word "pin" because we can mentally associate it with a set of homonyms (nail, peg, spike, bolt, and so forth) or with a set of acoustically similar words (pin, bin, tin, din), and so on. These other members of the paradigm do not actually occur in the moment of actualized speech, but remain *in potentia* in the mind of the speaker; the sets themselves are open-ended, randomly-ordered, and their acquisition depends upon verbal experience. These two relations—the syntagmatic and the paradigmatic—are virtually inseparable, according to Saussure, and both have equal influence on the ordering of speech. The analogy he uses to demonstrate the interplay of these relations is worth repeating here:

> . . . a linguistic unit is like a fixed part of a building, e.g., a column. On the one hand, the column has a certain relation to the architrave that it supports; the arrangement of the two units in space suggests the syntagmatic relation. On the other hand, if the column is Doric, it suggests a mental comparison of this style with others (Ionic, Corinthian, etc.) although none of these elements is present in space: the relation is associative.[6]

Language, then, consists of signs which have no validity or meaning outside the relations of equivalence and contrast with other signs in the system. This concept is relevant at all levels of linguistic description, and has come to take on importance beyond the science of language, as a means of describing any complex system decomposable into hierarchical and substitutable components—or, more broadly, as a means of describing the perceptual organization of phenomena. Roman Jakobson proposes that these relations correspond to two kinds of conceptualizing activity—the ability to order linearly and the ability to order associatively—and to the two orders of discourse in which one or another mode of organization predominates: metonymic and metaphoric discourse.[7] To the metaphoric mode belong, he says, lyric poetry, the works of the Romantic and Symbolist poets, Surrealist painting, and Freudian dream symbols; to the metonymic mode belong epic and realist narrative—to which list Roland Barthes has added popular novels and "newspaper narratives."[8] Claude Lévi-Strauss, in his famous chapter on the *bricoleur* in *The Savage Mind*, comments that science, too, is of a metonymic order—"it replaces one thing by another thing, an effect by its cause"—while art is of a metaphoric order.[9] Furthermore, Jakobson remarks, poetry is "the axis of simultaneities projected upon the axis of successions,"[10] while the novel, according to James Boon, is the axis of successions projected upon the axis of simultaneity—the narrative mode applied to a basically metaphoric vision of human action.[11] We are better prepared to understand the metaphoric than the metonymic mode, Barthes adds, because the "metalanguage" in which we carry out our study is itself metaphoric.[12]

The third concept which has been significant to the development of structural methodologies beyond linguistics is Saussure's distinction between *langue* and *parole*, a distinction roughly similar to Chomsky's more recent "competence" and "performance" and to the "code" and "message" of the information theorists. *Langue*, Saussure says, is the socially ordered aspect of speech; it is the

> sum of word-images stored in the minds of all individuals [who speak the same language] . . . a storehouse filled by all members of a given community through their active use of speaking [*parole*], a grammatical system that has a potential existence in each brain, or more specifically, in the brains of a group of individuals. For language is not complete in any speaker, it exists perfectly only within a collectivity . . . It is the social side of speech, outside the individual who can never create nor modify it by himself; it exists only by virtue of a sort of contract signed by the members of a community.[13]

Parole, on the other hand, is the "executed" aspect of language, the individual's momentary actualization of the collective potential of the *langue*. The two aspects are interdependent, Saussure says:

> Language is necessary if speaking is to be intelligible and produce all its effects; but speaking is necessary for the establishment of language, and historically its actuality always comes first . . . Speaking is what causes language to evolve; impressions gathered from listening to others modify our linguistic habits. Language and speaking [*langue* and *parole*] are then interdependent; the former is both the instrument and the product of the latter.[14]

Saussure's concept of the externality of the *langue* in relation to any particular individual and his clear disposition to give chief place to the communal contract of social values represented in the *langue* (even when he vigorously proposes the historical pre-eminence of speech) is determined at least in part by his understanding of Durkheim's psychological and sociological theories of the collective consciousness of the community and its power to order individual thought. It is important to those structural studies which focus on the constraints and laws which act to regularize and codify any system of signs, verbal or nonverbal. As we shall see later, the concept of the *langue* and the power of its ordering force has become more complex and controversial in recent years, and its current importance is its position at the center of a debate on the nature and status of the creative act.

Beyond linguistics, the influence of Saussure's structural descriptions of language was first felt by the Russian formalists, who learned of his work through Sergei Karcevski, a student of Saussure's who returned to Moscow in 1917. All of Saussure's major concepts appear in the work of the Formalists: the synchronic description of a work of art and the diachronic description of its place in the history of art;[15] the concept of the concrete, individual literary work (the *parole*) as it is related to the formal generic structure from which it arose (the *langue*);[16] the distinction between the syntagmatic or metonymic order of language and the paradigmatic or metaphoric order.[17] After 1917 the basic Saussurian dichotomies became a part of the methodologies of the Formalists, who in turn passed them along to the structuralists.

The young Russian theoreticians were not interested in the traditional questions of literary scholarship—What is the work about? Who wrote it? When? Why?—but with the urgent questions How is it made? What are its defining characteristics? What techniques account for its effect? To answer these questions they turned to the formal description of the literary work—and first (because many of them were linguists) to the phonological features of the piece of literature, to its actual physical manifestation.

Krystyna Pomorska sums up the large achievements of this early concern for the linguistic aspects of the work—studies of syntax, phonology, metrics:

> Many brilliant studies, particularly those on verse structure, resulted from such a tendency. During the early and later periods of the Opojaz [the Moscow School], the works of O. Brik, such as "Zvukovye povtory" ("Sound Repetitions," 1919) or "Ritm i sintaksis" ("Rhythm and Syntax"), Jakubinskij's "O zvukax stixotvornogo jazyka" ("On Sound in Verse Language," 1916), B. Tomasevskij's *Russkie stixoslozenie (Russian Versification*, 1923), and his articles later published as a book, *O stixe (On Verse*, 1929), Zirmunskij's *Vvedenie u metriku) Introduction to Metrics*, 1925)—all these studies showed not only how poetic language was constructed but also they simultaneously proved how poetic language differed from the nonpoetic, or as they phrase it, "practical language."[18]

The concern to distinguish poetic language from everyday language led in several important theoretical directions. In the work of Victor Shklovsky it produced the concept of *ostraneniye*, estrangement.[19] The difference between the esthetic and the ordinary, Shklovsky asserted, is that in ordinary experience our perceptions are "automatized," we learn to react habitually to certain signals in the environment without actually perceiving them, in order to employ our perceptive faculties with the greatest economy of effort.[20] In the esthetic experience, however, objects, phenomena, and ideas are made unfamiliar, difficult. "The process of perception is an esthetic end in itself," Shklovsky writes, "and must be prolonged." The devices which perform the function of making difficult, prolonging, or "estranging" the perceptual processes are the technical devices of art—specific to medium, often specific to genre within the medium. The search for the uniqueness of the literary language directed several Formalists to a concentration upon these devices. "The notion of 'technique,'" Eichenbaum remarked at one point,

> because it has to do directly with the distinguishing features of poetic and practical speech, is much more significant in the long-range evolution of formalism than is the notion of "form."[21]

Other studies in the *specifica* of literary language and literary form led to a marked concentration among the Formalists upon the "literariness" of literature, on the autonomy of art, on the *dominant* ("the focusing component of a work of art [which] rules, determines and transforms the remaining components.")[22] These larger, more theoretical concerns soon began to diffuse the early concentration on the physical structures of the work, leading to a more general concern with literature and with its historical and generic contexts. Eichenbaum, summing up the "formal method" in 1927, makes a clear statement of the new direction later Formalist studies were taking —from form to technique to function, from "literariness" to the relation between literature and life—and in his attempt to stave off the inevitable political interference makes an impassioned outburst against his own early work.[23] But the more "structuralist" enterprise came to an unfortunately early end, and the further development of Formalism was thwarted by the political suppression beginning as early as 1923, when Trotsky maintained that the Formalist approach to literature was incomplete, that it ignored the social context of the art work.[24] Another more pointed attack in the following year charged the Formalists with the "decadent" and "sterile" appreciation of art for art's sake. A few Formalists attempted compromise—Alexander Zeitlin argued that the contextual analysis of art could not be carried out until a more complete understanding of the inner workings of the piece of art itself had been achieved, and Shklovsky and Eichenbaum both attempted to present Formalism as a "scientific," objective study of data, compatible in its scientific concerns with Marxism. But neither tactic worked, and by 1929 the Marxist rout of the Formalists was nearly complete.[25]

While the Formalists paid the greatest amount of attention to the language and structures of poetry, they directed some study to narrative—particularly to the analysis of plot. Shklovsky's distinction between plot (*suzet*) and story (*fabula*) opened the way to a rhetorical understanding of the many devices by which plot distorts and estranges story, and to a perception that these devices are related to general devices of style.[26] In terms of the analysis of narrative structure, however, the most important work produced by the Formalist school was Vladimir Propp's *The Morphology of the Folktale*, published in Moscow in 1928. As Alan Dundes observes in his preface to the second English edition, the effect of Propp's provocative analysis of narrative can be measured in part by the number of studies to which it has given rise—and, it might be added, by the quality of critical speculation on the nature of narrative that it has generated.[27] Propp's avowedly synchronic undertaking—to provide a complete and objective morphological description of a type of tale, that is, to provide a formal definition of a genre—was new to folklore scholarship (new, indeed, to literary scholarship as a whole). Although he had two important predecessors (the French scholar Bedier and the Russian Veselovsky), whose works on invariant and variant story components dealt with the problem of narrative form, Propp's study of the formal features of story and their functional interrelationships was the first of its kind. His important contribution, which can be only briefly described here, is his typically Formalist proposal that the description of a tale's invariant structural features is a more appropriate mode of analysis than the description of the variable content which manifests the structure. He aimed to show that the *functions* (invariant actions) of the characters are the "recurrent constants" of the tale; that the number and type of these functions peculiar to the Russian fairy tale is limited (he distinguished 31 functions) and is governed by the laws of narrative logic which always produce an identical sequence of functions in the tale; and that all Russian fairy tales (as he defined the term) belong to one structural type. *The Morphology of the Folktale* includes the systematic description of the thirty-one narrative functions and the distribution of these functions among characters (or, more accurately, among *dramatis personae* or character types); and the configuration of sequences of functions ("moves") in patterns of end-to-end arrangement, embedded organizations, envelopment, and bifurcation.

Together with the other Formalists Propp insisted that the literary analyst should be concerned only with the tale itself and not with its historical, psychological, or cultural contexts. To the question "If all fairy tales are so similar in form, does this mean that they all originate from a single source?" Propp answers that the morphologist does not have a right to answer, that when he is finished with his formal analysis he should hand over his conclusions to a historian or should become a historian himself. And Propp, like most of the other Formalists, was more interested in what would now be called "surface-structure features" of the tale; what characterizes his analytical method is his emphasis on the syntagmatic plane of the story, following the chronological and linear ordering of the sequence of events. The model of the linear enchaining of narrative components in a syntactically ordered, rule-governed sequence of predictable patterns is precisely analogous to Saussure's description of the "axis of successions," the syntagmatic plane.

It is precisely these two characteristics—the Formalist limitation of focus to the work itself and the reliance on the temporal, linear analysis of the work—that have generated the greatest controversy around Propp's work and set him apart from the later structuralists. In a 1960 review of Propp's study, Claude Lévi-Strauss takes him to task on both counts: for his deliberate refusal to consider the "ethnographic context" which surrounded and produced the tales; and for his emphasis on the syntagmatic, temporally-ordered aspect of the narrative, an emphasis which, Lévi-Strauss observes, requires him to ignore other kinds of narrative organization—specifically the "deep" or "latent" structures which generate the surface features of the tale.[28] It is this deep structure, Lévi-Strauss argues, that creates and defines the events of the story; it can be represented, he says, by arranging the narrative events (or "mythemes") along a gridded matrix which shows not only their chronological, syntagmatic relations but their paradigmatic relations as well, the associative bonds that reveal the latent structure of binary oppositions underlying the surface structure features. The "principle of permanence" of narrative structure does not lie on the axis of successions, Lévi-Strauss says, but on the axis of simultaneity, where the generating force of the narrative is to be discovered.

Lévi-Strauss has demonstrated his paradigmatic analysis of mythic structure in two short articles, "The Structural Study of Myth" and "The Story of Asdiwal."[29] In "The Structural Study of Myth" he presents the complete model of deep-structural analysis, illustrated by a brief examination of the Oedipus myth. Lévi-Strauss' conception of myth is similar to Freud's understanding of dreams:[30] like dreams, myths are the articulation of unconscious cultural desires which are for some reason inconsistent with the conscious experience of the world. The myth presents an answer to the question "How are the unconscious wishes to be reconciled with conscious understanding?" by finding some sort of resolution between the two—a resolution which cannot be tolerated, perhaps cannot even be conceived, in real life. Structurally this resolution takes place along the two axes described by Saussure: the temporal axis of successive events in mythic story, and the a-temporal axis of associative patterns by which these events acquire meaning. In structural analysis, then, we are dealing with two kinds of time—the diachronic, non-reversible time of the story and the reversible synchronic time, the pattern that "explains the present and the past as well as the future." Deciphering myth, Lévi-Strauss says, is like deciphering music. In order to read an orchestra score, the melodic line must be read diachronically across the page, while the harmony must be understood synchronically, up and down the lines and spaces of the staff, in its chord structure. It is in the balance between harmonic pattern and melodic movement that music and language—or music and myth—are alike.

This analogy appears frequently in Lévi-Strauss' work; one of its earliest appearances is in "The Structural Study of Myth," where he argues that the meaning of the Oedipus story lies not in the developing melodic line (the plot line) of the story but in the latent structure of the narrative. This structure is found by reconstructing the "chordal" patterns, arranging the "mythemes" or story segments in columns (See fig. 1). These paradigmatic sets are generated by two pairs of deep structural

Kadmos seeks his sister Europa ravished by Zeus		Kadmos kills the dragon	
	The Spartoi kill each other		
			Labdacos (Laios' father) = lame (?)
	Oedipus kills his father Laios		Laios (Oedipus' father) = left-sided (?)
		Oedipus kills the Sphinx	
Oedipus marries his mother Jocasta			
			Oedipus= swollen-foot (?)
	Eteocles kills his brother Polynices		
Antigone buries her brother Polynices despite prohibition			

Figure 1 (from "The Structural Study of Myth.)

oppositions: the "overrating of blood relations" (incest) opposed to the "underrating of blood relations" (fratricide, patricide); and the killing of chthonian monsters so that man can be born from the earth (denial of autochthonous origin) opposed to club-footedness (persistence of autochthonous origin). By opposing the four columns in an analogical ration (column 4 is to column 3 as column 1 is to column 2) Lévi-Strauss finds that the myth displaces the original unanswerable question faced by the culture—born from one or born from two?—by the more answerable yet still troublesome question—born from different or born from same? The mythic narrative, then, functions as an attempt to resolve a basic contradiction in beliefs: to meet a dilemma on one level of experience by shifting the terms of the problem to another level, where a mediator is more readily found. The Oedipus myth provides a logical model for investigating and understanding man's origins in the natural world.[31]

In "The Structural Study of Myth" we find the "correction" to Propp's syntagmatic reading of narrative structure. In "The

Story of Asdiwal" we find the structuralist's answer to what he considers the Formalist's narrow approach. In this essay Lévi-Strauss retells a Tsimshian Indian myth of the birth and life history of Asdiwal, born to a human mother and bird-father. It is not the narrative events which Lévi-Strauss finds of interest in the story, however, but rather what Mary Douglas has called "the complex symmetry of different levels of structure," a series of oppositions which generate these events: the geographic, cosmologic, economic, and kinship oppositions. There are, then, at least four deep structural patterns in myth, the interrelations of which produce a highly symmetrical plot and system of character relationships united in a story with a fourfold logical significance. But Lévi-Strauss does not end his argument with this formal analysis of the narrative, for he assumes that kinship relations, relations of economic and geographic exchange, and relations of ritual and ceremony are of the same order as linguistic relations and narrative relations. All of the structures of a community demonstrate an essential identity, he says, although that identity may appear to be altered by one or a series of permutations, depending on the nature of the activity and its function in the lives of the people. In "The Story of Asdiwal" he goes on to discuss the relationship between the myth and the Tsimshian culture which produced it—a relationship which is not one of direct reflection but of "dialectic re-presentation," in that the institutions and ritual processes which occur in the myths are the very opposite of what happens in the actual life of the society. Mythic speculations, Lévi-Strauss says,

> do not seek to depict what is real but to justify the shortcomings of reality. . . . This step . . . implies an admission (but in the veiled language of the myth) that the social facts when thus examined are marred by an insurmountable contradiction.[32]

And yet the myth is functional in society; it is a logical model through which the community can resolve its contradictions and in terms of which it can see its relation to the natural world. This model, as Lévi-Strauss explains in the second volume of his *Mythologiques*, "renounces all external criteria" and tests its inductive observations only against its own deductive expectations (in this way, he wryly observes, it is exactly like our own modern science); it is a model which, through all its inversions and permutations, presents a stable universe capable of complete logical explanation. This notion reverberates through all his work. In *La Pensée sauvage* he treats the complex logical structures through which primitive people deal with the natural world, using elements of their environment for the purpose of classifying natural and social objects. In *Le Cru et le cuit*, the first volume of his monumental *Mythologiques*, he treats the transformations that occur when mythic structures are transmitted from culture to culture, having been retailored to answer the needs of a variety of communities. In this work and in the two volumes which follow it he is concerned to show how all of the myths he describes (187 in the first volume alone) are related through a set of regular, systematic permutations in a single mythic structure—which may be present in the myths themselves or in Lévi-Strauss' own mythic imagination. The question of the reality of the structures encountered in (or imposed on?) this complex mass of narratives is not really resolved in *Mythologiques*, although it frequently arises to plague the reader.[33] For Lévi-Strauss the question whether the mythic structures he perceives are the product of his vision or the mind of others is ultimately of little concern; the structures of myth reflect the structures of the mind of man—generic man—and those structures are common to us all. Hence the question whether his "myth about myths" represents his own thinking or the thinking of the natives through whom the myth originally came into being is of little moment.

In this sense Lévi-Strauss' structural understanding of the interaction between man and the physical world around him has gone beyond "structuralism" to a phenomenological understanding of the ways in which we create the structures that become so real that they in turn can be empirically assessed and measured. This double vision can most clearly be seen in *Tristes Tropiques*, where Lévi-Strauss reflects movingly upon the nature of ethnography, upon his own earlier conceptions and misconceptions of the Brazilian tribes he visited, and upon the meaning of those experiences for him now, in a post-war world. It can also be seen in *La Cru et la cuit*, as James Boon points out:

> For, always insisting that contents can only be known empirically (and then only as structured by the observer), he hopes to illuminate universal logical *processes*. It is not *what* his myths (analyses) say, it is *how* they derive what they say that counts most.[34]

It is in this way, Boon asserts, that Lévi-Strauss is like the Symbolist poets, whose dealings with the world are primarily dealings with themselves, with the metaphors that for them organize the metonymy of everyday existence. In *Tristes Tropiques* Lévi-Strauss attempts to establish a structural (metaphoric) ordering of what he has perceived, Boon says:

> But, like the Symbolist poems, these orderings are nowhere near "the thing itself." For the thing itself—these societies—cannot be grasped in and of itself, but can only be known indirectly across the fact of a relationship that is established between whatever that thing is and an observer. Well, then, however, on second thought, if there is a "society-thing" that *is*, it must itself be epistemologically grounded in some such observer-relation situation—hence the locus of Lévi-Straussian "structure," his rediscovery of subjectivity in the social sciences and the breakdown of observer/observed dualism, even in empirical investigations. Unable, then, to *know* the primal perfection, Lévi-Strauss determines to describe how he is unable to know it, and the result is *Tristes Tropiques*, an anti-ethnography.[35]

Lévi-Strauss' work has raised loud and frequently angry responses from his colleagues in anthropology, who are disturbed by his mode of classification (an almost unverifiable ordering which comes from the categories of a closed binary system), by the quality of his field work, and by what Edmund Leach has called the "oracular elegance" of his writing, which "wraps up profundity in verbal obscurity."[36] Other anthropologists, however, have been able to apply a Lévi-Straussian approach to a variety of mythic materials and to arrive thereby at new and interesting insights. In *Genesis as Myth*, for example, Leach works through the "logical categories" established in the narratives of the Biblical creation story, uncovering a structural pattern based on singleness and multiplicity; in "Lévi-Strauss in the Garden of Eden" he says that the structure is based on "isolated unitary categories such as man alone, life alone, one river, [which] occur only in ideal Paradise; in the real world things are multiple and divided; man needs a partner, woman; life has a partner, death."[37]

Lévi-Strauss' influence has moved beyond anthropology, however, and his analyses of myth have made a profound impact upon studies of narrative structure, particularly in France, where a bewildering variety of literary scholars, all with some interest in narrative structure, have for the last twenty years practiced one or another version of structuralism. To provide a rough sorting of this group, let me divide them into two "Schools": those who, following Lévi-Strauss, are concerned with deep or latent structures which shape the narrative at a level below the artist's conscious manipulation; and those whose studies have been to some extent influenced by Russian Formalism and who work primarily with surface structures consciously controlled by the artist for esthetic effect.

Alexander Greimas works with what he calls an "actantielle model," a generative approach which focuses on the processes by which the surface features of narrative are derived.[38] Following Lévi-Strauss closely, he argues that myth has three components: the armature (a narrative model consisting of all the variants); the message (the individual, actual manifestation of the myth); and the code (a formal structure constituted by a small number of "semantic categories" which account for all of the content selected to appear in a particular mythic universe). He begins his analysis at the level of formal syntactical components, dividing the narrative into two sequences: an opening and closing sequence ("contenu correle"), which is constituted by Propp's two major functions, *lack* and *lack liquidated;* and the central sequence ("contenu topique"), which provides the means whereby the narrative balance is restored and the liquidation of the initial lack comes about. Having established the narrative structure, he turns to the "contractual categories" that organize the whole of the story: "un jeu d'acceptations et de refus d'obligations."[39] These contractural relations undergo several transformations which alter the distribution of roles among characters: in one mythic form, he suggests, the traitor-son is transformed into a hero, while the father-victim is transformed into a traitor. He turns, finally, to the Lévi-Straussian notion of the generative, binary "codes," the resolution of which motivates the myth—life/death, raw/cooked, fresh/rotten. Greimas' analysis, then, like that of Lévi-Strauss, moves from the latent structure to the surface structure; unlike Lévi-Strauss, he is interested as well in understanding the syntactical relations among actual narrative sequences; again unlike Lévi-Strauss, he has no anthropological intrest in the relation between the culture and its myths, nor in finding structural homologies among several aspects of the culture.

Greimas does not himself attempt to deal with non-mythic narrative—understandably, since his method seems to preclude the possibility of conscious esthetic control on the part of the artist. For both Greimas and Lévi-Strauss, the code (Saussure's *langue*) dominates the creation of all messages; no deliberate deviation from the social and communicative norms established in the code are possible, because of its powerful controlling force. Julia Kristeva has observed that it is this belief in the dominance of the code that has set up the current dichotomy in structural studies. One phase of the study of man's use of signs is now over, she comments,

> that [phase] which runs from Saussure and Peirce to the Prague School and structuralism, and has made possible the systematic description of the social and/or symbolic constraint within each signifying practice.[40]

This difficulty derives, she suggests, from the linguistic model itself:

> established as a science in as much as it focuses on language as a social *code*, the science of linguistics has no way of apprehending anything in language which belongs not with the social contract but with play, pleasure or desire . . .[41]

An indication of this shift away from the *langue* was earlier apparent in the work of the Formalists, who were less concerned with the constraints of the code and more concerned with the devices by which the code was called into question, or "estranged."[42] In fact, for all of those whose attention is focused on literary works (rather than on myth, ritual, or folktale), the question of the formal and functional differences between esthetic discourse and everyday discourse is always a crucial one. It concerned Eichenbaum and Tomashevsky and most of the other Formalists; it concerned Jan Mukarovský, perhaps the most productive of the group of Prague linguists and literary critics that began to meet in the early 1920s. As René Wellek has pointed out, the Formalists had been associated with the Russian Futurist poets, and the esthetic theories they developed were at least in part a defense of Futurist experiments with language;[43] when in 1932 the Prague School began its attacks on a journal which advocated grammatical norms of purity and correctness, it was following in the path of earlier Formalist interests, attempting to differentiate the literary codes from the codes of everyday language. Mukarovský's stylistic studies of norm and deviation (or organization and deformation) provide a clear record of the interest of the Prague School in understanding the effect of the code on the unique individual message and underscore their emphasis on the surface-structure features of the language.[44] We might observe here that the Prague and Formalist efforts illustrate the fact that structural studies have developed different emphases and methods in order to deal with the problems inherent in different kinds of texts: literary texts, marked by significant (and regular) deviations from the norms of speech, must be analyzed with tools designed to deal with small-scale surface features; popular narratives, folktales, and myth, on the other hand, demand an analysis which is capable of dealing with a large number of similar texts, with larger structural patterns, with deep structure. Because the Formalists and the Prague School linguists were involved with the innovations of contemporary poetry and with unique literary texts, they concentrated their attention on the problems of manifest rather than latent structure.

This same concern for surface structure marks the work of the second "school" of French structuralists—led by Roland Barthes and Tzvetan Todorov—who are indebted for their method to the Formalists rather than to Lévi-Strauss.[45] Both Barthes and Todorov (who has translated the basic Formalist texts into French) have reworked Shklovsky's notion of plot (*suzet*) and story (*fabula*) into the concept of story (*histoire*) and discourse (*discours*). The story is the basic narrative logic, the sequence of events as they would have happened in "natural," chronological time, objectively re-enacted. The discourse is the narrative as we read it, its temporal sequences reordered, its action filtered through one or another point of view, its expression governed by the speech of a narrator.[46] The literary narrative is always a product of such reworking, Todorov notes; an artist never is content simply to reproduce the story in its "natural" state but is led to restructure it for certain esthetic ends, carefully calculating the effect of the literary devices he uses.[47] It is the esthetic restructuring that both Barthes and Todorov attend to—a restructuring that is carried out under the conscious control of the artist, a restructuring that is not governed by latent forces operating at an unconscious level but is rather the result of the deliberate deployment of devices chosen for their effect.

For Todorov, as for the Formalists, the esthetic effect is the result of a carefully designed attempt to interrupt the reader's patterns of expectation—to deviate from the regular norms of literary discourse and the discourse of everyday speech. In his brief analysis of *Les Liaisons dangereuses*, for instance, he finds violations of the expected logical, social, and narrative orders at each level of the work. In fact, he observes,

> The story owes its very existence to the violation of order. If Valmont had not transgressed the rules of his moral code (and that of the novel) we would never have seen his published correspondence, nor that of Merteuil: the publication of their letters is a consequence of their circumstances, which are not due to chance, as one might believe. The entire story, in effect, is justified only in so far as it is a punishment of misrepresentation. If Valmont had not been false to his earlier self, the book would never have existed.[48]

Barthes' work with narrative structure is similar in that he is concerned to describe the formal components of the literary work. Basing his analysis of narrative on the Proppian notion of function, he divided the *histoire* into two parts, functions and actions, both of which combine hierarchically to become narration (or *discours*) at the surface level of the work.[49] The functions are of two sorts—metonymic plot events ("cardinal functions") and metaphoric "indexical" functions (descriptions, setting, etc.). Cardinal functions move the story forward in a cause-effect sequence, Barthes proposes; indexical functions, on the other hand, are the "chord" structure of the work, the metaphoric echoes that provide "thematic" support for the plot. Further, these functions may be "open" or "closed" (Barthes calls these kernels—*noyaux*—and catalysts—*catalyses*), leading onward into alternative courses of action or embellishing an already existing movement.[50] It seems clear that Barthes' understanding of the "cardinal" and "indexical" functions is based on Saussure's model of the syntagmatic and paradigmatic axes of language—the same model from which Lévi-Strauss' structural analysis of myth arises. In fact, while the two modes of analysis are apparently quite dissimilar—they do, after all, work on very different levels of the text—they employ the same logical operations: those operations of syntactic and paradigmatic ordering that mark all structuralist activities.

Barthes' recent work in the larger domain of sign theory and signification has probably attracted more attention than his earlier studies of narrative structure, which are more explicitly "structural." Insofar as his criticism distinguishes between the systematic form of a text and its message, it is in the mainstream of structuralism; as it turns to the questions of sign and significance, to modes of signification, to the nature of knowing through signs and knowing signs—in these ways Barthes' work becomes more specifically semiotic rather than structural.[51] What is the difference? A semiotic theory attempts to understand signs and their use in the social world; it was suggested by Saussure as a science which would take as its subject the whole human system of meaningful signs and would contain linguistics as one of its divisions. As a theory, semiotics is broadly and powerfully explanatory, for it subsumes within itself a variety of explanations specific to certain aspects of communication: syntactic, semantic, pragmatic, meta-linguistic, and meta-communicative.[52] Structuralism, on the other hand, is an explanation of just one of these aspects—the syntactic relation of signs to one another in a regular and structured system—and the production of that sign system by its makers and users. Structuralism, then, is a part of semiotics, just as linguistics is a part of semiotics, and it is frequently useful to distinguish between the two.

But it is becoming increasingly more difficult these days to define the limits of structuralism, for the early, primarily formal concern with syntactic systems has given way to a larger apprehension of the total semiotic model—to an understanding of the relationships among the sematic, syntactic, and pragmatic axes of the communicative event. And at the same time, the assumption that all human intercourse is basically code-dominated is a major concern, and the structures of deviating patterns—the notion of deviation itself—has become the subject of much structuralist debate.

As structural methods are employed in other disciplines—in psychology, in biblical studies, in history—new understandings of the range and limitations of its explanatory abilities will be achieved, and each new application will continue to "reinvent" the fundamental structuralist questions: What are the basic patterns of events and action in human time, and how do they acquire meaning? What are the constraints that require particular choices at particular moments? How may the codified, obligatory rules of the *langue* be violated? How are these violations ordered and understood? While these questions remain at the center of discussions on literary and mythical texts, and on the texts of cultural artifacts, structuralism as a theory and as a methodology will remain very much alive.

NOTES

1. Richard Macksey and Eugenio Donato, eds., *The Structuralist Controversy* (Baltimore: Johns Hopkins Press, 1972), p. ix.
2. Ferdinand de Saussure, *Course in General Linguistics* (New York: McGraw-Hill, 1959).
3. John Lyons, *Introduction to Theoretical Linguistics* (Cambridge: Cambridge University Press, 1971), p. 46.
4. Saussure, *Course*, p. 80.
5. For a clear, precise discussion of *syntagmatic* and *paradigmatic* activity, see Lyons, *Introduction*, pp. 70-81; also see Roland Barthes, *Elements of Semiology*, tr. Annette Lavers and Colin Smith (Boston: Beacon Press, 1970), pp. 58-88, and Saussure, *Course*, pp. 122-27.
6. Saussure, *Course*, pp. 123-24.
7. Jakobson, "Deux Aspects du langage et deux types d'aphasie," in *Temps moderne*, No. 188, January 1962, pp. 853 ff.
8. Barthes, *Elements*, p. 60.
9. Jakobson, "Linguistics and Poetics," in Thomas A. Sebeok, ed., *Style in Language* (Cambridge, Mass.:MIT Press, 1960), p. 358.
10. Claude Lévi-Strauss, *The Savage Mind* (Chicago: University of Chicago Press, 1970), pp. 24-25.
11. James A. Boon, *From Symbolism to Structuralism: Lévi-Strauss in a Literary Tradition* (New York: Harper and Row, 1972), p. 105. I am grateful to Barbara Babcock-Abrahams, whose discussions of metaphor and metonymy have been helpful here.
12. Barthes, *Elements*, p. 61.
13. Saussure, *Course*, pp. 13-14. Also see Barthes, *Elements*, pp. 13-34; and Lyons, *Introduction*, pp. 51-52.
14. Saussure, *Course*, p. 19.
15. See Juri Tynianov, *Arxaisty i novatory* (Leningrad, 1929). A chapter of this important work, translated into English, appears in L. Matejka and K. Pomorska, eds., *Readings in Russian Poetics* (Cambridge, Mass.: MIT Press, 1971), pp.68-78. For a complete review of the Formalists' work, see Victor Erlich, *Russian Formalism: History and Doctrine* ('S-Gravenhage: Mouton, 1955).
16. Roman Jakobson and Petyr Bogaterev, "Die Folklore als eine besondere Form des Schaffens," *Donum Natalicium Schrijnen* (Nijmegen-Utrecht, 1929), pp. 900-913.
17. Jakobson, "Deux aspects du langage et deux types d'aphasie."
18. Pomorska, *Readings in Russian Poetics*, pp. 174-75.
19. Victor Shklovsky, "Art as Technique," in Lemon and Reis, eds., *Russian Formalist Criticism: Four Essays* (Lincoln: University of Oklahoma Press, 1965), pp. 3-57.
20. Shklovsky, pp. 11-13.
21. Eichenbaum, "The Theory of the Formal Method," in *Russian Formalist Criticism*, p. 115.
22. Roman Jakobson, "The Dominant," in *Readings in Russian Poetics*, p. 82.
23. In Chapter 5 of *Literature and the Revolution* (New York: Russell and Russell, 1957), Trotsky denounces the Formalists for their concentration upon the "literariness" of literature.
25. See Erlich, *Russian Formalism,*pp. 96-115.
26. Shklovsky, "Art as Technique," p. 57. See also Boris Tomashevsky, "Thematics," in *Russian Formalist Criticism*, pp. 66-78.

27. Vladimir Propp, *The Morphology of the Folktale* (Austin: University of Texas Press, 1970), p. xi.
28. Lévi-Strauss, "L'Analyse morphologique des contes russes," *International Journal of Slavic Linguistics and Poetics*, III (1960), pp. 141-43.
29. "The Structural Study of Myth" appears in R. De George and F. De George, eds., *The Structuralists from Marx to Lévi-Strauss* (Garden City: Doubleday, 1972), pp. 169-94. "The Story of Asdiwal" may be found in Edmund Leach, ed., *The Structural Study of Myth and Totemism* (London: Tavistock, 1969), pp. 1-48.
30. Boon, *From Symbolism to Structuralism*, pp. 179-81.
31. Cf. Octavio Paz, in *Claude Lévi-Strauss, An Introduction* (Ithaca: Cornell University Press, 1970), p. 31:

    In moral terms: the parricide is atoned for by incest; in cosmological terms: to deny autochtony (to be a *complete* man) implies killing the monster of the earth. The defect is atoned for by excess. The myth offers a solution to the conflict by means of a system of symbols which operate as do logical and mathematical systems.

32. "The Story of Asdiwal," p. 30.
33. For a discussion of the issues involved here, see Alan Dundes, "From Etic to Emic Units in the Structural Study of Folktales," *Journal of American Folklore*, 75 (1966), 95-105.
34. Boon, *From Symbolism to Structuralism*, p. 136.
35. Boon, p. 141.
36. Leach, *The Structural Study of Myth and Totemism*, p. xvi. On Lévi-Strauss' field work, see Leach, *Claude Lévi-Strauss* (New York: Viking Press, 1970), pp. 11-12.
37. Leach, "Lévi-Strauss in the Garden of Eden: An Examination of Some Recent Developments in the Analysis of Myth," *Transactions of the New York Academy of Science*, Ser. II, Vol. XXIII, No. 4 (February 1961), 386-96.
38. A. J. Greimas, "La Structure élémentaire de la signification en linguistique," *L'Homme*, IV, No. 3 (1964); *Sémantique structurale* (Paris: Larousse, 1966); *Du sens, essais sémiotiques* (Paris: Seuil, 1970).
39. Greimas, "Éléments pour une théorie de l'interprétation du récit mythique," *Communications,* 8 (1966), p. 45.
40. Julia Kristeva, "The Speaking Subject," *Times Literary Supplement*, Oct. 12, 1973, p. 1249.
41. Ibid.
42. For a discussion of ways in which the code may be questioned, see Jakobson, "Linguistics and Poetics," p. 356.
43. René Wellek, *The Literary Theory and Aesthetics of the Prague School* (Ann Arbor, 1969), p. 20.
44. See Jan Mukarovský, "Standard Language and Poetic Language," in Paul L. Garvin, *A Prague School Reader in Esthetics, Literary Structure, and Style* (Publications of the Washington Linguistic Club), pp. 19-35.
45. Tzvetan Todorov, *Littérature et signification* (Paris: Larousse, 1966); "Les Registres de la parole," *Journal de psychologie normale et pathologique*, 3 (1967); *La Grammaire du Decameron* (The Hague: Mouton, 1969); Roland Barthes, "Linguistique et littérature," *Langages*, 12 (1969), *Writing Degree Zero* (London: Cape, 1967), *Mythologies* (Paris: Seuil, 1957), *Essais critiques* (Paris: Seuil, 1964). Another important writer in this group is Claude Bremond, "Le Message narratif," *Communications*, 4 (1964), "Morphology of the French Folktale," *Semiotica*, II, No. 3 (1970).

46. Boris Uspensky, in *The Poetics of Composition*, tr. Zavarin and Wittig (Berkeley: University of California Press, 1973), describes point of view as those devices which articulate the basic structure of the story, providing for the surface-structure effects.
47. Todorov, "Les Catégories du récit littéraire," *Communications,* 8 (1966), p. 139.
48. Todorov, "Les Catégories," p. 150.
49. Barthes, "Introduction a l'analyse structural des recits," *Communications*, 8 (1966), 1-27. Seymour Chatman, an American structuralist, offers an interesting application of Barthes' methods in "New Ways of Analyzing Narrative Structure with an Example from Joyce's *Dubliners*," *Language and Style*, 4 (1970), 3-36.
50. Claude Bremond (in "Le Message narratif," *Communications*, 4 [1964], pp. 4-32), argues similarly that the structure of a story is composed of a series of "bifurcations," narrative choices which may be exploited by the artist.
51. See especially *Elements of Semiology*, in which Barthes argues that structuralism is a methodology subsidiary to semiotics.
52. The larger study of semiotics would take us to the works of Charles Sanders Peirce (*Selected Writings*, ed. J. Buchlev [New York: Harcourt Brace, 1940]) and Charles Morris (*Signs, Language and Behavior*, [New York: Prentice-Hall, 1946]). Jakobson's review of the functions and metafunctions of discourse is also useful ("Linguistics and Poetics," in *Style in Language*), and Gregory Bateson's "A Theory of Play and Fantasy," in *Steps to an Ecology of Mind* (New York: Ballantine, 1972), pp. 177-93, adds a socio-linguistic perspective.

WHY FROGS ARE GOOD TO THINK AND DIRT IS GOOD TO REFLECT ON

BARBARA BABCOCK-ABRAHAMS

There's rosemary, that's for remembrance.
Pray you, love, remember.
And there is pansies, that's for thoughts.[1]

CLAUDE LÉVI-STRAUSS' repeated assertion that certain animals are singled out as symbolic or totemic creatures not because they are "good to eat" or "good to prohibit" but because they are "good to think" (*bonnes à penser*) has met with a response not dissimilar to Ophelia's song: "a document in madness."[2] There is more commonality here than madness, and there is a method to their madness which I'd like to explore. In Ophelia's mad speech, Shakespeare draws upon and comments upon a highly developed Renaissance system of classification—the language of flowers—which sets up correspondences between natural species and human emotions or states of mind. So it is hardly happenstance that Lévi-Strauss in writing about primitive systems of categorization—"the logic of the concrete"—echoes Ophelia's metaphoric equivalence between thoughts and pansies in his punning title, *La Pensée sauvage*—a pun which is unfortunately lost in the translation *The Savage Mind*, and in the elimination of the original dust jacket illustration of pansies

Ms. Babcock-Abrahams teaches English, folklore, and critical theory at the University of Texas, Austin. She has published several structural analyses of narrative, both folk and literary, and recently edited a book of essays on anti-structural processes and phenomena, *The Reversible World: Essays on Symbolic Inversion*.

with wild faces. Like Ophelia's speech, *La Pensée sauvage* is about and is itself an example of the whole matter of assorting human beings and natural elements into fixed categories, and "then organizing the major part of collective existence around that assortment" (Geertz 1972:26). It is also about—as its punning title dramatically illustrates—the metaphoric confusion of categories, the deliberate creation of ambivalence or ambiguity by evoking in one word two different orders of experience.

Nor is it surprising that in his concern with man's passage from natural instinct to cultural self-awareness, Lévi-Strauss repeatedly discusses the logic of classification. Perhaps the first essential procedure for understanding one's environment is to introduce order into apparent chaos by classifying. And since "our survival as human beings depends upon our use of social categories which are derived from cultural classifications imposed on the elements of nature" (Leach 1970:30), it is not surprising that classification has long been "the prime and fundamental concern of social anthropology" (Needham 1963:viii). *La Pensée sauvage* (1962, trans. 1966), however, epitomizes a new and specific, i.e., a "structural" concern with classification. It began in 1962 and 1963 with the publication of Lévi-Strauss' *Le Totémisme aujourd'hui* and of Needham's translation of the Durkheim and Mauss paper "*De quelques formes primitives de classification.*" Since then key essays and monographs on the subject, such as Leach's "Animal Categories and Verbal Abuse" (1964), Mary Douglas's *Purity and Danger* (1966), Beidelman's work on Nuer category systems, Turner's analysis of Ndembu ritual and cosmology in *The Forest of Symbols* (1967) and *The Ritual Process: Structure and Anti-Structure* (1969), Tambiah's "Animals are Good to Think and Good to Prohibit" (1969), and most recently Needham's collection of essays on dual symbolic classification, *Right and Left* (1973), have brought classification to the foreground of attention and have aroused awareness of related problems concerning the mechanisms whereby conceptual categories are set up, preserved, and mediated.

All of these works are "structural" in several respects. In the first place, they regard culture as "mutually understood systems of communication" (Leach 1958:78-79). Each of these conceptual systems is seen as a structured arrangement of categories, a language, and may be analyzed as such. And as in structural linguistics, to which this form of anthropological analysis is indebted, the analytical focus is relational, being directed toward relationships among different cultural systems and among categories within any given system.[3] Further, since any description of the world must discriminate categories in the form "p is what *not*-p is not" (Leach 1964 and 1969), and since every category system is based on the principle of difference, such primitive logic is seen as intrinsically binary. But, as Leach points out, if the logic of our thought leads us to distinguish *we* from *they*, how can we bridge the gap and establish social, economic, and sexual relations with the *others* without throwing our categories into confusion? The usual answer is that mediation is achieved through the introduction of a third category such as amphibian, which is ambiguous or anomalous in terms of the ordinary categories of land and water animals. Such abnormal middle forms are regarded as dangerous and powerful and are typically the focus of taboo and ritual observance (Cf. Leach 1969:10-11). Thus all these studies of classification, through their relational emphasis, implicitly or explicitly raise questions regarding the role of ambivalent or interstitial items in classificatory schemes and the social and cognitive value of ambiguity.

Primitive Classification, published in 1903, was the first sociological study to deal solely and explicitly with the origins and cultural expressions of categories and with the interdependence of social relations and cosmological ideas. Its methodological procedure of "seeing a certain range of facts in their totality, as composing in a systematic fashion a whole of which the parts cannot be adequately comprehended in isolation from each other" (Needham 1963:xxxiv), was to become characteristic of the *Année sociologique* school and much later of structuralism generally. The major criticism of Durkheim and Mauss is that they posit a causal connection between social structure and symbolic classification and regard society as the cause or model of the classificatory system without ever considering logical alternatives to this approach, such as the possibility that "social organization . . . is itself an aspect of the classification" (Needham 1963:xxvi) and that classification is perhaps an innate faculty of the human mind. Its faults aside, their work is theoretically and methodologically significant to later studies of totemism and classification generally.

Lévi-Strauss' *Totemism* evidences the influence of the *Année sociologique* while at the same time offering an alternative to causal and functional explanations of totemism, i.e., of the identification of natural categories with social groups are expressed in terms of food prohibitions or taboos. In his concern with the fundamental passage from the naturally given to the culturally created, "the dialectical process by which [an] apotheosis of ourselves as human and godlike and other than animal is formed and re-formed and bent back upon itself" (Leach 1970:34), he explicitly singles out Rousseau as the founder of cultural anthropology and credits him with "an extraordinarily modern view" of this crucial transition (Lévi-Strauss 1962a:101). "Rousseau's thesis, as elaborated by Lévi-Strauss, is that man can become self-conscious—aware of himself as a member of a we-group—only when he becomes capable of employing metaphor as an instrument of contrast and comparison" (Leach 1970:35):

> It is only because man originally felt himself identical to all those like him (among which, as Rousseau explicitly says, we must include animals) that he came to acquire the capacity to distinguish *himself* as he distinguishes *them*, i.e., to use the diversity of species as conceptual support for social differentiation . . . a logic operating by means of binary oppositions and coinciding with the first manifestations of symbolism (Lévi-Strauss 1962a:101).

This demonstration in *Totemism* and later in *La Pensée sauvage* that totemism is a universal instance of "the social use of metaphor"[4] provided a fruitful alternative interpretation both to *universalist* explanations implying, à la Lévy-Bruhl, that totemic beliefs express a "childish" mentality once characteristic of all mankind and to *particularist* explanations based on functionalist propositions that special interests are attached to animal and plant species of, say, economic value (Leach 1970:39 and Lévi-Strauss 1962a: *passim*). Thus when a savage says that

> the members of his clan are descended from bear but those of his neighbour's from eagle, he is not giving forth with a bit of illiterate biology [or mental confusion]. He is saying, in a concrete metaphorical way, that the relationship between his clan and his neighbour's is analogous to the perceived relationship between species (Geertz 1967:29).

Or, as Lévi-Strauss puts it, such totemic taxonomies are "based on the postulate of a homology between two systems of differences, one of which occurs in nature and the other in culture" (Lévi-Strauss 1966a: 25).

At first glance Lévi-Strauss seems to reverse the Durkheim

—Mauss thesis that "the first logical categories were social categories" (Durkheim and Mauss 1963:82). Yet despite the fact that he says that the binary logic of classification is an intrinsic property of the human mind, he refuses to satisfy the readers' expectation that "he will eventually label some level of experience—such as 'social organization' or 'ideas'—primary or causal" (Boon:129). As a consequence, however, of his constant reference to the "*esprit humain*" and his repeated insistence that certain species are "good to think," he has been accused of idealism, mentalism, and intellectualizing the natives—creating "cerebral savages."[5] While he does indeed argue that savage thought is just as aesthetically and intellectually sophisticated as our own though it is expressed in a different system of notation, i.e., in concrete rather than abstract terms, he also states that "there is no real intrinsic basis for distinguishing between the sensory-concrete and the intellectual-abstract" (Boon:117). Given his critical concern with the mutual complementarity of *sens/esprit*, of empiricism and idealism, it is probably futile to try (as many have) to define his work in either/or terms. Perhaps the fairest assessment is to say that his main contribution consists in the "creation of a definite place for human intellect in the explanation of social reality . . . without thereby denouncing a materialist perspective" (Scholte:652).

But above all what excites anthropologists and scholars in other disciplines about Lévi-Strauss' analyses of classification is its translatability to the analysis of any conceptual schema. By deciphering the principles behind the universal logical process of analogizing between analytically separate orders of experience, he makes it possible to compare systems as apparently different as Australian totemism and Indian castes. Or, within a given culture,

> one can even move between different levels of social reality—the exchange of women in marriage, the exchange of gifts in trade, the exchange of symbols in ritual—by demonstrating that the logical structures of these various institutions are, when considered as communication systems, isomorphic (Geertz 1967:30).

And yet the very applicability of his method and the facility with which he applies it leads even Clifford Geertz to fear that he has created an "infernal cultural machine." That may be, but we can still learn a lot from it.

Paradoxically, the very scholars who have criticized his algebra of possibilities and his disregard of empirical facts have demonstrated how well his logic of analogy works when it is applied to well-documented social and cultural systems. Leach's "Animal Categories and Verbal Abuse" and Tambiah's "Animals are Good to Think and Good to Prohibit" are cases in point. Both analyses correlate three series of categories: marriage and sex rules, spatial or ecological categories, and animal categories with attendant dietary rules, and convincingly validate Lévi-Strauss' assertion that even in such non-totemic societies as contemporary England, Burma, and Thailand there is an empirical connection between marriage rules and eating prohibitions and that this connection is neither causal nor utilitarian but metaphorical. All these societies have food taboos concerning dogs, who, though animal, are treated as humans, live in our houses, eat our food, and are given names, and the prohibition against eating dogs is parallel or logically equivalent to our negative attitudes toward incest. Such terms which occupy relationally equivalent positions in our category systems may be metaphorically substituted for each other as, for example, in the use of "bitch" as a form of verbal abuse, or in the Thai ritual in which, to expiate the negative consequences of incest, the guilty parties eat as dogs do, out of a tortoise shell on the ground.

In sum, these and other studies of classification bear out Lévi-Strauss' suggestion that

> ideas and beliefs of the "totemic" type particularly merit attention because, for the societies which have constructed or adopted them, they constitute codes making it possible to ensure, in the form of conceptual systems, the convertibility of messages appertaining to each level, even of those which are so remote from each other that they apparently relate solely to culture or solely to society, that is, to man's relations with each other, on the one hand, or, on the other, to phenomena of a technical or economic order which might rather seem to concern man's relations with nature (Lévi-Strauss 1966a:90-91).

They also suggest that one of the distinctive features of the "totemic operator"—be it a dog or a frog—is the mediation between nature and culture. In fact, previous studies of such category systems have, by emphasizing the priority of either the natural or the cultural, failed to understand the metaphoric nature of totemism, which is "pre-eminently the means (or hope) of transcending the opposition between them" (Lévi-Strauss 1966a:91).

Despite the objections of "scientific" social scientists, this "aesthetic" concern with the dynamics of the social use of metaphor is particularly appropriate if we remember that

> metaphor is one of the richest results of the interaction between the structure of the human mind and its perceived world, [and] can illuminate far more than the specific information it is designed to reveal. It can provide a key to the interpretation of a whole work, or even a whole era or culture (Deese:215).

And given this preoccupation with metaphor, the analytic fascination with that which is ambiguous or "betwixt and between" categories logically follows, for analogies and all figures based on resemblance are inherently ambiguous. In fact, it is this aspect of metaphorical thought that makes possible the expression and re-expression of varieties of social and cultural truth. Or, as Mary Douglas states in her exciting study of anomaly and ambivalence, *Purity and Danger*:

> any given system of classification must give rise to anomalies, and any given culture must confront events which seem to defy its assumptions. It cannot ignore the anomalies which its scheme produces, except at the risk of forfeiting confidence. That is why, I suggest, we find in any culture worthy of the name various provisions for dealing with ambiguous or anomalous events (1966:52).

While Douglas and others use the terms anomaly, ambiguity, and ambivalence as if they were synonyms, strictly speaking they are not. An *anomaly* is "an element which does not fit a given set or series" (Douglas 1966:50). Twins, for example, are a social anomaly, a classificatory embarrassment, and in many societies are either killed at birth or given divine status. *Ambiguity* is a character of statements such as puns or jokes "capable of two interpretations"; similarly a word, concept, or item of behavior is *ambivalent* when it belongs to two or more frames of reference. For Mary Douglas anomaly, ambiguity, and ambivalence are all forms of "dirt," i.e., "matter out of place." "Dirt is the by-product of a systematic ordering and classification of matter, in so far as ordering involves rejecting inappropriate elements" (Douglas 1966:48).

Dirt may be reacted to negatively or positively or ignored. More specifically, there are at least five cultural strategies for dealing with ambiguity (after Douglas 1966:52-53).

1. *Ambiguity is reduced by settling on one or other interpretation*. For example, a monstrous birth may threaten the defining lines

between human and animal, but if it can be labelied an event of a peculiar kind the categories can be restored. So, as Evans-Pritchard describes, the Nuer regard monstrous births as baby hippopotamuses, accidentally born to humans. With this labelling the appropriate action is clear and they are gently laid in the river where they belong.

2. *The existence of an anomaly can be physically controlled*. Thus in some West African tribes the rule that twins should be killed at birth eliminates a social anomaly.

3. *A rule of avoiding anomalous things affirms and strengthens the definitions to which they do not conform*. That which is tabooed, such as Leviticus' abomination of crawling things, is the negative side of the pattern of things approved. Leach represents as follows the relationship between ambiguity and taboo, in which *p* represents a particular verbal category and ~*p* the 'environment' of *p* from which it is desired to distinguish *p*. If by a fiction we impose a taboo upon any consideration of the area of overlap, we can persuade ourselves that *p* and ~*p* are wholly distinct and our logic of binary discrimination is satisfied (Leach 1964:36):

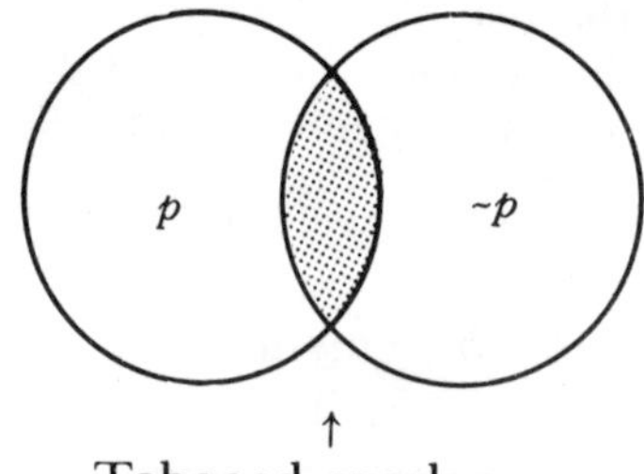

↑
Tabooed overlap
"Both *p* and ~*p*"

Thus all exudations of the human body which are ambiguously *of* and *not of* the self are universally the objects of intense taboo.

4. *Anomalous events may be labeled dangerous*. Attributing danger is one way of putting a subject above dispute and enforcing conformity.

5. *Ambiguous symbols can be used in ritual*, for the same ends as in poetry and mythology, *to enrich meaning or call attention to other levels of existence*. Lévi-Strauss' analyses of myth and Douglas' and Turner's of ritual demonstrate again and again how myth and ritual, by using symbols of anomaly, can incorporate evil and death along with goodness and life into a single, grand, unifying pattern.

The presence of such anomalous symbols in religious rites throughout the world and thus the connection between dirt and sacredness is what is referred to in the theological notion of "the ambiguity of the sacred." It is this concept, first formulated by Robertson Smith in his *Religion of the Semites* (1889) and then taken up by Durkheim in *The Elementary Forms of the Religious Life*, that lies behind Mary Douglas' comprehensive discussion of ritual pollution. The symbolic communication of religion between the spheres of man and the supernatural

> often involves vehicles normally kept separated. In our own society the ambiguous symbolic attributes of Christ (man/god), Mary (mother/virgin) and the eucharistic feast [communion/cannibalism] are examples of this. In Nuer society oxen, and objects substituted for oxen, are vehicles for such mediation and synthesis, being male yet not partaking of active sexuality. They combine opposed attributes which give them a character betwixt-and-between Spirit and Creation, of neither and of both. Such ritual involves a paradox: it establishes contact between two spheres so that these may be better separated (Beidelman 1966:454).

And, insofar as ritual involves ambiguity, it also partakes of dirt, which may just be another word for paradox.

The essence of Douglas' thesis regarding dirt is that it, like totemism, is to be understood metaphorically rather than functionally or psychologically. Dietary prohibitions and the labeling of certain animals as "unclean" make sense in relation to a systematic ordering of ideas (a classificatory system) as exemplified by the abominations of Leviticus. What is most suggestive about her "suggestive" approach[6] to dirt is that "it implies two conditions: a set of ordered relations and a contravention of that order" (Douglas 1966:48). Dirt is good to reflect on because "reflection on dirt involves reflection on the relation of order to disorder, being to non-being, form to formlessness, life to death" (Douglas: 16).

What Douglas describes as the dynamic of "system" and "dirt" or "form" and "formlessness," Turner terms "structure" and "anti-structure." In *The Forest of Symbols* (1967), *The Ritual Process* (1969), and most recently in *Dramas, Fields, and Metaphors* (1974) he has brilliantly demonstrated the operation of this dynamic in ritual processes and symbols as well as in non-ritual phenomena such as play and literature. Elaborating upon Van Gennep's tripartite model of the *rite de passage*, Turner examines the ritual process as consisting of separation, margin or *limen*, and reaggregation. *Liminality* is an anti-structural state, "betwixt and between" all fixed points of classification. One is, for example, no longer a boy and not yet a man and is therefore structurally if not physically invisible.

This position of structural or status ambiguity is expressed in a variety of ambivalent and anomalous symbols such as grotesque half-human, half-animal masks, males in female dress, and the like. Turner describes these exaggerated figures as a primordial mode of abstraction—the ambiguous creature becomes an object of reflection, teaching neophytes to distinguish between the different factors of reality by confusing them. This analysis of the cognitive value of ambiguity is quite similar to Koestler's formulation of the "bisociation of two matrixes"—the perception of a situation or idea in two self-consistent or mutually incompatible frames of references—which he, like most proponents of metaphor, sees as basic to abstract and creative thought.

While there is much to be said about Turner's analysis of ritual and classification proper, what is most useful for the non-anthropologist is his extension of the notion of liminality and the analysis of anti-structure to a wide variety of antinomian phenomena and counteractive patterns of culture. In so doing he has greatly increased our understanding of the "betwixt-and-between" and the symbolic inversions of our social and cultural categories. Like Leach and Mary Douglas he elucidates the order of things by making sense of disorder, i.e., of the universal processes by which people symbolically confuse, invert, and subvert their systems of classification.[7]

If we understand dirt and disorder we can understand why the tales of Trickster are so popular and universal. Trickster, as both good *and* evil, both creator *and* destroyer, is the very personification of human ambiguity, of the transcendence of all opposition.[8] So perhaps Lévi-Strauss is neither a madman nor an idealist but simply the latest incarnation of Trickster, inviting us—as do all celebrations of ambiguity—to turn round and confront the categories on which our culture has been built up and "recognize them for the fictive, man-made, arbitrary creations they are" (Douglas 1966:200). Like Trickster he baffles, deceives, amuses, and at the same time teaches us a great deal. In *Mythologiques* he carries his preoccupation with classification to the logical conclusion of creating his own cosmology, a "metamyth" of New World mythology in which frogs figure centrally as mediators, as keys to systems of signification.[9]

Frogs are *naturally* very "good to think" because "their perceptible reality permits the embodiment of ideas and relations conceived by speculative thought on the basis of empirical observations" (Lévi-Strauss 1962a:89). For example, they are seasonal (temporally discontinuous); they are vocal; they are notoriously ambivalent in that they bridge the water/land opposition and undergo observable metamorphosis, and so forth. In short, "frogs present a wealth of potential distinctive features for sets of contrasts" (Boon:158), and as natural mediators can operate mythically as points of transition between different frames of reference or classificatory sets, between nature and culture. Given this natural multivalence, it is no wonder that frogs are frequently encountered in New World mythology and in Lévi-Strauss' metamyth. It is, as Boon points out, a moot question whether the frogs' repeated appearance across space is indicative of diffusion or of independent invention, for

> from a structural point of view they would have *persisted* throughout diffusion for the same reason that they might have been independently *invented*: the reason being their capacity to act as operators in the establishment and maintenance of meaning (Boon:158).

For this reason we continue to engage in "raids on the bestiary"[10] to express our cosmology and social order. "Classification is a pre-requisite of the intelligible ordering of experience, but if conceptual categories are reified, they become obstacles rather than means to [an] understanding and control of both physical and social reality" (Hamnett:387). And if we define culture as the ability to construct categories and to revise and transcend them, then culture, as Rousseau asserted, is defined by metaphor, for metaphor is "the means by which we establish and re-arrange the agreed-upon orders of our natural and cultural environments" (Abrahams:3). In conclusion, the most salutary lesson we can learn from metaphor and from these anthropological studies of its social use is

> how to live a conceptual contradiction, how happily to situate ourselves at the metaphoric nexus where incompatibles are said to be fused and not fused (Cullers:220).[11]

NOTES

1. *Hamlet*, Act IV, Scene v, ll. 175-77. It was Edmund Leach who first pointed out, in *Claude Lévi-Strauss* (New York: Viking Press, 1970), p. 88, that the dust jacket of *La Pensée sauvage* with its illustration of wild pansies purposely recalled these Shakespeare lines.
2. Ibid., l. 178.
3. For the original discussion of structural analysis in linguistics and anthropology see Claude Lévi-Strauss, *Structural Anthropology* (New York: Basic Books, 1963), Chapter 2.
4. This phrase is taken from the title of David Sapir's and Christopher Crocker's collection of essays on totemism and related classificatory problems entitled *The Social Use of Metaphor* (unpublished manuscript).
5. "The Cerebral Savage" is the title of a fine discussion by Clifford Geertz of Lévi-Strauss' analysis of *pensée sauvage*, published in *Encounter* (1967), pp. 25-32.
6. The suggestiveness and analytical usefulness of Douglas' and Leach's classificatory approach has been borne out in innumerable anthropological studies of which only a few are cited here. More recently, however, it has proved equally illuminating of the nature of riddles and social stereotypes, as exemplified in Roger D. Abrahams' "Man as Animal," in *Hard Words* ed., Bruce Jackson and Diane Christian, in press, and Ian Hammett's "Ambiguity, Classification and Change: The Function of Riddles," *Man* 2:3 (September 1967), pp. 379-92.
7. For general discussions of symbolic inversion see my Introduction and Victor Turner's "Comments and Conclusions" to *The Reversible World: Essays on Symbolic Inversion* (Ithaca: Cornell University Press, in press).
8. For analysis of Trickster and his tales in terms of Turner's and Douglas' models see my " 'A Tolerated Margin of Mess': Trickster and His Tales Reconsidered," *Journal of the Folklore Institute* (1974).
9. For Lévi-Strauss' treatment of frogs see *Mythologiques*, especially Vol. II, Pt. II and Vol. III, pp. 57ff.
10. This phrase is taken from Paul Ricoeur's recent discussion of "Metaphor and the Main Problem of Hermeneutic," *New Literary History* 6:1 (Autumn, 1974).
11. I am indebted to Victor Turner and Roger Abrahams for innumerable illuminating conversations about dirt and disorder, and to Susan Wittig and the students in our first structuralism class for prompting me to develop those ideas.

BIBLIOGRAPHY

Abrahams, Roger D.

"Man as Animal." In Bruce Jackson and Diane Christian, eds., *Hard Words*. In press.

Babcock-Abrahams, Barbara.

1974 " 'A Tolerated Margin of Mess': The Trickster and his Tales Reconsidered," *Journal of the Folklore Institute*. In press.

Introduction. *The Reversible World: Essays on Symbolic Inversion*. Ithaca: Cornell University Press. In press.

Beidelman, T. O.

1961 "Hyena and Rabbit." *Africa* 31:1, 61-74. Reprinted in Middleton, ed., *Myth and Cosmos*, 287-301.

1966 "The Ox and Nuer Sacrifice: Some Freudian Hypotheses about Nuer Symbolism," *Man* 4 (December), 453-69.

1968 "Some Nuer Notions of Nakedness, Nudity, and Sexuality," *Africa* 38, 113-32.

Boon, James A.

1972 *From Symbolism to Structuralism: Lévi-Strauss in a Literary Tradition*. New York: Harper and Row.

Bulmer, Ralph

1967 "Why Is the Cassowary Not a Bird? A Problem of Zoological Taxonomy among the Karam of the New Guinea Highlands," *Man* 2:1 (March), 5-25.

Crocker, J. Christopher and David Sapir

The Social Use of Metaphor. Unpublished manuscript.

Culler, Jonathan

1974 "Commentary," *New Literary History* 6:1 ("On Metaphor"), 219-29.

Deese, James

1974 "Mind and Metaphor: A Commentary," *New Literary History* 6:1 ("On Metaphor"), 211-18.

Diamond, Stanley

1974 "The Myth of Structuralism." In Ino Rossi, ed., *The Unconscious in Culture: The Structuralism of Claude Lévi-Strauss in Perspective*. New York: E. P. Dutton and Co., Inc.

Douglas, Mary

1957 "Animals in Lele Religious Symbolism," *Africa* 27, 47-58. Reprinted in Middleton, ed., *Myth and Cosmos*, 231-48.

1966 *Purity and Danger: An Analysis of Concepts of Pollution and Taboo*. Middlesex, England: Penguin Books.

1970 *Natural Symbols: Explorations in Cosmology*. New York: Pantheon Books.

Durkheim, Emile

1965 *The Elementary Forms of the Religious Life*. Translated by Joseph Ward Swain. New York: The Free Press. (Originally published 1915).

Durkheim, Emile and Marcel Mauss

1963 *Primitive Classification*. Translated and edited by Rodney Needham. London: Cohen and West. (Originally published 1903).

Firth, Raymond.

1966 "Twins, Birds and Vegetables: Problems of Identification in Primitive Religious Thought," *Man* 1 (March), 1-17.

Geertz, Clifford

1966 "Religion as a Cultural System." In Michael Banton, ed., *Anthropological Approaches to the Study of Religion*. London: Tavistock, 1-46.

1967 "The Cerebral Savage," *Encounter* 28:4, 25-32.

1972 "Deep Play: Notes on a Balinese Cockfight," *Daedalus* (Winter), 1-38.

Hamnett, Ian

1967 "Ambiguity, Classification and Change: The Function of Riddles," *Man* 2:3 (September), 379-92.

Hayes, E. Nelson and Tanya, eds.
1970 *Claude Lévi-Strauss: The Anthropologist as Hero*. Cambridge, Mass.: M.I.T. Press.

Koestler, Arthur
1964 *The Act of Creation*. New York: Dell Publishing Company.

Leach, Edmund
1958 "Magical Hair." *The Journal of the Royal Anthropological Institute* 88:2, 147-64. Reprinted in Middleton, ed., *Myth and Cosmos*. New York: The Natural History Press, 1967, 77-108.
1961 *Rethinking Anthropology*. New York: Humanities Press, Inc.
1964 "Anthropological Aspects of Language: Animal Categories and Verbal Abuse." In E. J. Leneberg, ed., *New Directions in the Study of Language*. Cambridge, Mass.: M.I.T. Press, 23-63.

Leach, Edmund, ed.
1967 *The Structural Study of Myth and Totemism*. London: Tavistock Publications.
1967 "Brain-Twister." *The New York Review of Books* 9:6 (October 12), 6, 8, 10. Reprinted in Hayes and Hayes eds., *Claude Lévi-Strauss: The Anthropologist as Hero*, 123-32.
1969 *Genesis as Myth and Other Essays*. London: Jonathan Cape.
1970 *Claude Lévi-Strauss*. New York: The Viking Press.

Lévi-Strauss, Claude
1962 *Totemism*. Translated by Rodney Needham. Boston: Beacon Press.
1962 *La Pensée sauvage*. Paris: Librairie Plon.
1963a *Structural Anthropology*. New York: Basic Books.
1963b "The Bear and the Barber," *Journal of the Royal Anthropological Institute* 93, Part I:1-11.
1964 *Mythologiques I: Le Cru et le cuit*. Paris: Plon.
1966a *The Savage Mind*. Chicago: The University of Chicago Press.
1966b *Mythologiques III: L'Origine des manières de table*. Paris: Plon.
1969 *The Raw and the Cooked: Introduction to a Science of Mythology, I*. New York: Harper and Row.
1971 *Mythologiques IV: L'Homme nu*. Paris: Plon.
1973 *From Honey to Ashes: Introduction to a Science of Mythology, II*. New York: Harper and Row.

Marc-Lipiansky, Mireille
1973 *Le Structuralisme de Lévi-Strauss*. Paris: Payot.

Middleton, John, ed.
1967 *Myth and Cosmos: Readings in Mythology and Symbolism*. New York: Natural History Press.

Needham, Rodney
1963 "Introduction." Durkheim and Mauss, *Primitive Classification*. London: Cohen and West, vii-xlviii.
1973 *Right and Left: Essays on Dual Symbolic Classification*. Chicago: The University of Chicago Press.

Radcliffe-Brown, A.R.
1965 *Structure and Function in Primitive Society*. New York: Free Press. (First published, 1952).

Ricoeur, Paul

"Metaphor and the Main Problem of Hermeneutics," *New Literary History* 6:1 ("On Metaphor"), 95-110.

Scholte, Bob

1973 "The Structural Anthropology of Claude Lévi-Strauss." In John J. Honigmann, ed., *Handbook of Social and Cultural Anthropology*. Chicago: Rand McNally and Company, 637-716.

Steiner, George

1967 "Orpheus with his Myths," *Language and Silence*. New York: Atheneum, 239-50.

Tambiah, S.J.

1969 "Animals are Good to Think and Good to Prohibit," *Ethnology* VIII: 4 (October), 243-59.

Turner, Victor W.

1967 *The Forest of Symbols: Aspects of Ndembu Ritual*. Ithaca: Cornell University Press.

1969 *The Ritual Process: Structure and Anti-Structure*. Chicago: Aldine.

1974 *Dramas, Fields, and Metaphors: Symbolic Action in Human Society*. Ithaca: Cornell University Press.

AN EXERCISE IN STRUCTURAL HISTORY:

An Analysis of the Social Criticism of Claude Lévi-Strauss

DAVID PACE

THE TYPICAL TOURIST visiting the Musée de la Marine in Paris is apt to be attracted to the intricately carved models of ancient French galleons or to the remains of Napoleon's imperial barge. In the presence of these concrete vestiges of Gallic naval ambition, visitors often ignore the panoramas of French seaports which line the walls. If someone does stop for a moment to admire these works by the eighteenth-century painter Joseph Vernet, he or she may well be charmed by these busy portraits of the commercial life of the ancient regime. But Vernet's strict academic style, his obsession with detail, and his intense formalism seldom appeal strongly to sophisticated modern tastes.

Yet, in his radio conversations with the critic Georges Charbonnier in 1959, the eminent French anthropologist Claude Lévi-Strauss singled out Vernet's paintings for praise. They were, he insisted, among the very few works of art with which he could still establish a rapport:

> I can well imagine (he said to Charbonnier) that I could live with these paintings and that the scenes which they represent would become more real for me than those which surround me. The value which these scenes have for me is related to the fact that they offer

David Pace has been teaching intellectual history in the History and West European Studies Departments at Indiana University in Bloomington since 1971. His dissertation was entitled "The Bearer of Ashes: Claude Lévi-Strauss and the Problem of Cultural Relativism," and he is presently completing a historical study of Lévi-Strauss' attitudes towards Western and non-Western peoples.

> me the means to relive that relationship between the sea and the earth which still existed in that epoch; this human settlement, which did not completely destroy but rather ordered the natural relations of geology, geography, and vegetation, thus restores a special reality, a dream world where we can find refuge.[1]

A passage such as this poses very difficult problems for the intellectual historian. On the one hand, it is a bit of information concerning one of the most important figures in contemporary French thought. Lévi-Strauss went out of his way to express this unconventional view about a relatively minor artist. And evidence concerning his world-view and values is crucially important to any historian attempting to unravel the threads of post-World War II European culture. As the founder of structural anthropology, Lévi-Strauss has been immensely important in the development of structural methodologies, and his work has been influential not only in anthropology but in areas as far removed from his own discipline as literary criticism and philosophy. Moreover, through *Tristes Tropiques*, his popular autobiographical account of his expedition to Brazil in the 1930's, and through various pamphlets, essays, and interviews during the 1950's and 1960's, Lévi-Strauss has become one of the foremost defenders of the value of primitive cultures. Both his structural methodology and his polemics against Western ethnocentrism have had a great impact, not only within France but throughout Europe, the Americas, and India as well.

Yet it is extremely difficult for the historian to deal with passages such as Lévi-Strauss' comments on Vernet. These statements about the eighteenth-century painter contain no explicit propositions about the human condition, social existence, or values of Western civilization from which the historian can directly extract Lévi-Strauss' world-view. There is only an expression of personal preference, buttressed by a few descriptive passages.

Some historians in the past have ignored texts such as this, concentrating instead on explicit statements of principle, theory, or ideology. But this approach tends to distort the thought of the past. It is quite possible that only part of an author's world-view is—or can be—expressed in terms of straightforward propositions; entire complexes of ideas and values may be presented only indirectly in descriptive passages, isolated personal comments, or literary flourishes. Moreover, implicit expressions of belief may have a much greater impact on the public than explicit arguments set forth directly in the text.

Of course there have always been historians acutely aware of this problem. But when they actually set about analyzing passages such as the one quoted above they have found it difficult to move beyond impressionistic judgments. The historian who has been immersed in Lévi-Strauss' work, for example, may have a very strong intuition that certain patterns which occur in the passage on Vernet can be found elsewhere in the anthropologist's writings. But how is this "gut" reaction, this impression of similarity and pattern, to be translated into a clear, explicit theory of Lévi-Strauss' work and of his position in the development of the modern French world-view? And how is this theory to be presented in such a way that it can be rationally evaluated by other historians?

There is no absolute solution to this dilemma. As long as the historian deals with the realm of meanings, he or she will always be involved at least to some extent with personal interpretations. But there are now methods available through which this process of interpretation can be made much more explicit and systematic. The techniques of structural analysis developed by Lévi-Strauss himself can be applied to historical materials to produce a more clearly ordered methodology. By analyzing the formal structure of a thinker's work and specifying the oppositions which exist within it the intellectual historian can minimize the impressionistic elements in his or her work.

This process must begin by treating the description not as an isolated statement about Lévi-Strauss' reaction to Vernet's painting but as a part of a larger structure of discourse. Within this larger structure oppositions between various elements emerge more clearly and the broader significance of the original passage can be put into perspective.

Thus the first step in such a structural analysis is to compare Lévi-Strauss' description of Vernet's seaports with other passages from his writings. Fortunately, in *Tristes Tropiques* Lévi-Strauss has provided an image of twentieth-century seacoasts which stands in stark contrast to his description of the scenes depicted by Vernet:

> . . . the charms which I identify with the sea [he wrote] are denied us today. Like an aging animal, whose carapace thickens, forming an impermeable crust about his body which no longer allows the

> epidermis to breathe and thus accelerates the process of senescence, most European countries allow their coasts to become cluttered with villas, hotels, and casinos. Whereas in other times the littoral offered a foretaste of the ocean's solitude, it becomes a kind of front line where men periodically mobilize all their forces for an assault on freedom; and yet they deny the value of this freedom by the very conditions under which they have agreed to take it. On the beaches the sea once delivered us the fruits of thousands of years of agitation and produced an amazing gallery in which nature classified herself with the avant-garde; but today under the trampling crowds, the seashore merely serves as a place for the disposal of rubbish.[2]

The concrete differences between Lévi-Strauss' descriptions of these two types of seacoast are immediately obvious. In the world depicted by Vernet man kept within his ecological niche. The seaport was a "human" environment; its relationship with geology, geography, and vegetation was "natural." Man did not destroy the world around him but brought order and reason to the landscape and to his own life through a reciprocal interaction with the environment.

By contrast the seashore of the twentieth century is a desolate place. Lévi-Strauss described it in terms of invertebrate, not human metaphors. Culture has become dominant over nature, and the harmony which once existed between man and his environment has been destroyed. Things no longer have their place; the world is "cluttered," "crowded"; the beaches are "trampled." The otherness of the sea has been destroyed and is no longer a source of mystery. Man has succeeded in taming nature, but by his very success he has lost his vitality. He no longer has room to breathe. He has become aged.

"Coded" into the concrete differences between these two descriptions of the relationship between man and the sea is a series of abstract distinctions which reveal a portion of Lévi-Strauss' world-view. Oppositions between the past and the present, order and chaos, harmony and conflict, nature and culture, and beauty and ugliness are superimposed upon one another in these descriptions and serve to define Lévi-Strauss' universe.

But a structural analysis cannot stop at this point. The kinds of abstract distinctions which underlie this concrete contrast of seacoasts can also be found hidden within other sets of descriptions in Lévi-Strauss' writings. *Tristes Tropiques*, for example, is a book of landscapes, and its lyrical descriptions of the seas, forests, deserts, and farmland which Lévi-Strauss encountered in his travels serves as a framework through which he can express his view of the world. The work is in effect a kind of mythology of environments in which geographical contrasts serve as concrete metaphors to express subtle conceptual differences.

Lévi-Strauss' environmental mythology may be reduced to four basic situations in which nature and culture interact: (1) the wilderness of the South American interior; (2) the quasi-civilized areas of North and South America; (3) the crowded Indian subcontinent; and (4) the traditional farmland of Europe. In his descriptions of these four environments Lévi-Strauss established a grid of contrasts through which he could express both distinctions of fact and differences of value. And by specifying the differences between his concrete descriptions and comparing them with the differences already established in the contrast between the two seacoasts the historian can make the general structure of Lévi-Strauss' universe a little clearer.

The most striking of Lévi-Strauss' four environments is that of the South American interior. Here was nature raw and untouched, "a virgin and solemn landscape which seemed to have preserved intact the image of the carboniferous era for millions of centuries."[3] Lévi-Strauss had dreamed of such an exotic environment when he was a student in Paris, but once he actually entered the interior of Brazil he found it impossible to relate to his surroundings. "The European traveler," he wrote, "is disconcerted by this landscape which does not fit any of his traditional categories."[4] This was a world which was too alien, too much Other. There was no place within it for man—or at least for Europeans. Westerners could destroy this environment, but they could not learn to inhabit it.

The wilderness Lévi-Strauss discovered in Brazil stood in sharp contrast to the civilized areas of the Americas. In these regions nature had become so completely subjugated to human purposes that it had lost almost all of its otherness. The Europeans who had migrated to the New World had succumbed to the Faustian temptation to dominate their environment and had sacrificed the purity of nature in their quest for power. The once seemingly limitless resources of the Americas had been so exploited that nature itself became twisted and perverted.

This destruction of the otherness of nature took two forms. The most obvious was the ruthless exploitation of the soil through capitalist agriculture, such as Lévi-Strauss observed in the cane fields of the Antilles. Here he discovered "a nature so piteously subdued that it had become an open-air factory rather than countryside."[5] The other form of exploitation was visible in those areas where man had misused the environment for a few years and then abandoned it to weeds and erosion. In Brazil, in the Northeastern United States, and even in the Rockies Lévi-Strauss discovered a nature robbed of all its richness, "not so much wild as degraded." In these regions man had destroyed the wildness of nature but he had not yet firmly established his own hegemony. Thus thousands of acres of the New World were covered with a monotonous vegetation which "preserves beneath a facade of false innocence the memory and the form of former struggles."[6]

This destruction of nature was even more evident in the third environment which Lévi-Strauss described in *Tristes Tropiques*, the world of the Indian subcontinent. When he visited India and Pakistan in 1950 he found exploitation which exceeded that of the Americas. In the Americas some trace of nature remained; in Asia only man was visible.

Lévi-Strauss believed that in India and Pakistan urban civilization had reached its most destructive stage. The pressure of population growth had long since destroyed the possibility of a harmonious balance between man and nature. The forests had been destroyed, and for centuries the manure which should have been used to fertilize the soil had been consumed as fuel. Nature as a thing independent of man's designs and purposes had disappeared completely.

Moreover, the density of population had compromised human relations as well. The great religious and philosophical systems of India had been unable to prevent the complete dehumanization of personal interactions. In the streets of Calcutta, where he recognized the unbridgeable gap which existed between himself and the crowds of beggars, and at the shrine of Kali, where the crippled and sick merged with vendors of religious objects to form a sea of struggling bodies, Lévi-Strauss saw the total dehumanization of man. As he later wrote, "Never, without a doubt—except in the concentration camps —have human beings been so thoroughly confused with butcher's meat."[7]

In this crowded world even the biological nature of man

himself was denied by culture. The bodily functions of human beings were limited as much as possible. Lévi-Strauss was shocked at the workers' districts in India, where two or three were crammed into tiny cells. Meals were communal and armed police constantly patrolled outside the company barracks. The only parallel which he could find to this way of life was the force-feeding of geese on French farms:

> . . . each [goose] had been shut up in a narrow box and reduced to the condition of digestive tube. Here was exactly the same thing, with this double difference, that in the place of geese I was looking at human beings, and in the place of fattening them, the preoccupation was with making them thin. But in both cases the breeder recognized in his charges only one activity, desirable in the first case, inevitable in the second: these dark, ill-ventilated cells did not lend themselves to rest, or to pleasure, or to love. No more than moorings on the bank of a communal sewer, they arose from a conception of human life reduced solely to the exercise of the excretory function.[8]

Thus for Lévi-Strauss Asia was not a land of mystery and exoticism. It exhibited the same destructive tendencies as the West. "I saw," he wrote in *Tristes Tropiques*, "prefigured before my eyes an Asia of worker's cities and cheap apartments, which will be the Asia of tomorrow and which will repudiate all exoticism . . ."[9]

Ironically, after Lévi-Strauss had traveled to the Americas and toIndia in search of an ideal human environment, he discovered it at home. It was the centuries-old farm land of Europe which offered him an ideal model of man's proper relationship with nature. In these areas—and in certain parts of Central and South America which have been settled for centuries—there had been a compromise between nature and culture which allowed man to live in harmony with his surroundings and with his fellow men. Here one finds neither the chaos of pure nature nor the chaos of unreasoned exploitation; rather there is a deeper order born of centuries of accommodation between man and the soil:

> But even the most rugged landscapes of Europe present a kind of order, of which Poussin was the incomparable interpreter. Go to the mountains: observe the contrast between the arid slopes and the forests; the stages by which they rise above the meadows, the diversity of shades due to the predominance of this or that species of vegetation caused by the exposure or the slope—it is necessary to have traveled in America to realize that this sublime harmony, far from being a spontaneous expression of nature, is evidence of

long-sought-for agreements achieved through collaboration between the site and man. Man naively admired the traces of his own past achievements.[10]

This idyllic environment was the result of centuries of continuous habitation. In the exploited areas of the Americas, Lévi-Strauss wrote, the land "has been occupied by man long enough for him to plunder it, but not so long that a slow and continuous cohabitation has raised it to the rank of a landscape."[11] In South Asia man has had time to accommodate to the environment, but the pressure of population has prevented the establishment of true harmony with nature. But in the settled countryside of Europe and parts of Latin America, man has learned to live at nature's own speed; he has become a part of his environment. In these regions man has learned the passive virtues—patience, adaptation, the wisdom of generations. The Faustian drive for knowledge and power has been kept within its proper limits.

It is clear that these descriptions are not just literary ornamentation, that they express some of Lévi-Strauss' basic reactions to the world. The contrasts between these environments carry much of the message in *Tristes Tropiques*, and these contrasts may be expressed in terms of sets of oppositions along two axes. Along the first axis the environments are arranged according to their proximity to Pure Nature or Pure Culture. This can be expressed in a simple diagram:

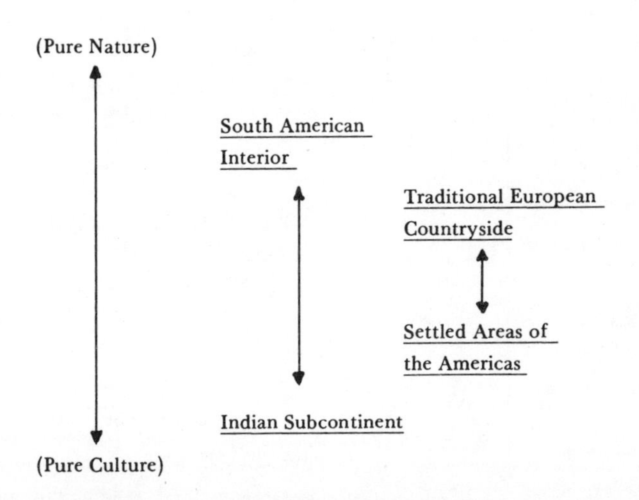

In this diagram the South American interior represents the total dominance of the environment by nature, whereas the Indian subcontinent is at the opposite pole, the point at which nature is completely overwhelmed by culture. Neither is suitable for meaningful human life, since man is a creature who exists at the intersection of nature and culture. But in Lévi-Strauss' schema they define the extreme limits of human existence.

This extreme contrast is repeated on a smaller scale in the opposition between the traditional European countryside and the more recently settled portions of the Americas. (South American Interior : South Asia :: Traditional European Countryside : Settled Areas of the Americas.) But the diagram is not symmetrical. The European environment occupies the middle position, equidistant from nature and culture, and it represents a viable compromise between the two. The exploited environment of the Americas is a false mediation, because the demands of nature have been ignored. In these regions man has objectivized nature and treated it as a kind of booty to be seized in rapid raiding parties. So in these regions the mediation between nature and culture is only apparent and is not an authentic response to the human condition.

This opposition between the settled, traditional lands of Europe and Latin America and the exploited areas Lévi-Strauss encountered elsewhere in the Americas is repeated along the second axis of Lévi-Strauss' typology:

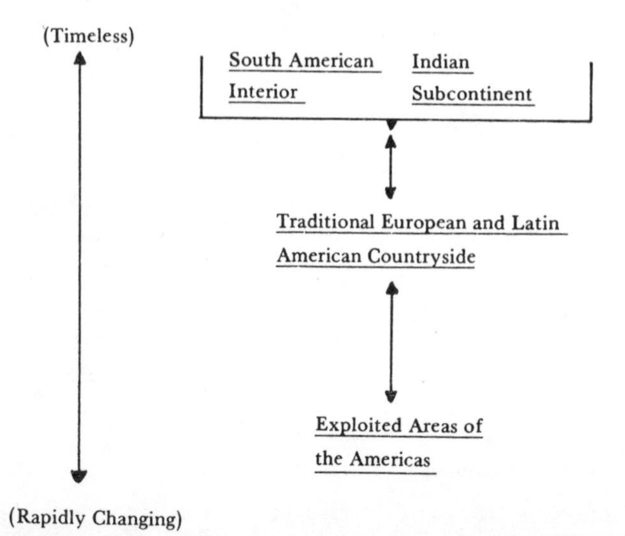

Along this axis the empty interior of South America and the overcrowded Indian subcontinent are lumped together at one extreme, since neither environment changes—at least on the human scale of time. These environments are not suitable places for human habitation because they allow man no power to change his situation. At the opposite end of the spectrum are the exploited areas of the Americas, where change has occurred rapidly but has been immensely destructive. And, once again, the traditional countryside of Europe and certain parts of Latin America is a suitable mediation between undesirable extremes—in this case between changelessness and destructive change.[12]

Thus, Lévi-Strauss' description of environments in *Tristes Tropiques* contains some very important statements about his view of man's place in the cosmos and of the value of change. Moreover, this information reproduces and amplifies that contained in the opposition between Vernet's seacoasts and those of the twentieth century. In both sets of concrete oppositions Lévi-Strauss was clearly seeking a mediation between nature and culture and between stagnation and destructively rapid change. In these descriptions conflict, rapid progress, and the entire Faustian ideal of radical control over nature were treated negatively; Lévi-Strauss idealized instead the image of the wise peasant, who lives in harmony with the cycles of nature. Many of these same values recur in Lévi-Strauss' discussions of art with Charbonnier. This time the contrasts are expressed within a clearly historical framework, but they may still be seen as a transformation of the kinds of oppositions we have been discussing.

In the passages on the history of art from Charbonnier's *Conversations with Claude Lévi-Strauss* the first crucial opposition is that between the grand landscapes of the sixteenth-century painter Nicolas Poussin and the more humble scenes painted by the late-nineteenth-century Impressionists. Like the paintings of Vernet, the landscapes of Poussin carried Lévi-Strauss back to an idealized, pastoral, pre-industrial Europe, where artists "were only interested in noble and grandiose landscapes. They had to have mountains, majestic trees, etc." By contrast, the painters of the late nineteenth century "were satisfied with far less: a field, some cottages, a few puny trees . . ."[13] The Impressionists and their contemporaries lived in a world which was aesthetically impoverished in comparison with that of earlier centuries, and their paintings reflected that fact:

> Thus, however much admiration we may have for the Impressionists [Lévi-Strauss wrote], it would not seem to be doing them an injustice to say that their work is the painting of a society which is in the process of learning that it must give up many things which had been available to previous epochs; this ennoblement of the suburban landscape, its rise to the level of pictorial representation can, perhaps, be explained by the fact that these things were always beautiful, even though no one had recognized it before; but more importantly it was because the grand landscapes which inspired Poussin were less and less accessible to the men of the nineteenth century. Soon they will exist no longer. Civilization is now destroying them more or less everywhere, and man must learn to content himself with more modest pleasures.[14]

Thus it was the legitimate historical role of the Impressionists, according to Lévi-Strauss, to teach Europeans "to be satisfied with the small change of a nature which has disappeared forever."[15] But even this compromise was not lasting, for the suburban landscapes ennobled by the Impressionists did not last very far into the twentieth century. The Cubists were forced to carry their work one step farther and ignore nature altogether. They recognized that they lived in "a world surrounded by culture and the products of culture," and so they attempted to find beauty in human artifacts. In so doing they were facing honestly—and perhaps even courageously—the reality of modern civilization.[16]

Lévi-Strauss might have argued that the Abstract Expressionists have simply carried this development of artistic subject matter to its logical conclusion by eliminating any direct reference to the non-cultural from their paintings, but he refused to take this position. If beauty had to be "non-objectivized" he preferred to bestow it not upon a canvas but rather on certain carefully chosen natural objects, such as shells or pebbles. Thus he suggested a return to the Surrealists' notion of the "objet trouvé," calling for the artist to place the last remnants of nature on display as works of art. For Lévi-Strauss it was better to cling to the last shred of nature than to give oneself over completely to cultural artifice.[17]

This transition from the classical landscape painters to the Abstract Expressionists recapitulates in many ways the oppositions we have encountered elsewhere in Lévi-Strauss' work.

These descriptions of art may be reduced to a simple linear, historical progression:

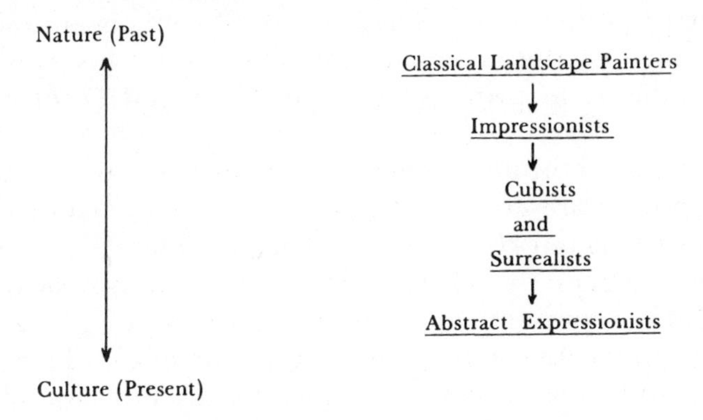

Like the totally culturalized societies of the Indian subcontinent, Abstract Expressionism has divorced itself completely from all contact with nature. And the artistic world of the Cubists and Surrealists—like the exploited areas of the Americas—has contact with only the shattered fragments of nature left over after man has ruthlessly exploited his environment.

There is, however, a fundamental difference between the structure of this discussion of art history and that of Lévi-Strauss' typology of environments. The latter is based on geographical distinctions at a single moment in time, and in this scheme the best environment—that of the traditional peasant —lies between the unsatisfactory extremes. In his discussion of art, however, the contrasts are projected onto an axis of historical development. And on this axis the most valuable state lies at one extreme; the earliest form of art—that of the classical landscape painters—is clearly the most desirable. The past is preferable over the present in the development of art, just as the seacoasts of Vernet's time are more desirable than those of the twentieth century.

But there is a second set of crucial structural oppositions in Lévi-Strauss' discussions of art. These revolve around his distinction between "primitive" and "civilized" art, and in this typology both classical and modern European art are grouped together at one extreme and compared to non-Western art.

Lévi-Strauss saw three fundamental differences between "primitive" and "civilized" art. First, in urban civilizations such as that of modern Europe there has been a tendency to establish a division between the artist and the social group—a division which does not exist, Lévi-Strauss argued, in primitive societies. In "civilized" societies only small groups of connoisseurs share the language of the artist and can understand his symbolic representations; in primitive societies the language of art is shared by all.[18]

Secondly, Lévi-Strauss argued that urban civilizations tend to create a more representational art than do primitive cultures. In societies such as our own there has been an attempt to possess rather than suggest the object of art. For the primitive the object which is to be represented has a meaning which extends beyond its merely physical existence. The object is the nexus of magical, religious, and social forces which the artist attempts to capture through his symbols. The artist in "civilized" cultures, by contrast, has systematically attempted to de-mystify the object, to destroy what Lévi-Strauss called the "super-abundance of the object." Exact physical reproduction has been gained through the sacrifice of the broader social and religious meaning of art.[19]

These two differences between primitive and "civilized" art are closely related. In primitive societies art is a collective phenomenon, and so the object takes on the collective meanings of the social group. But as the production and consumption of art have become more individualized, "necessarily and automatically, the semantic function of the work tends to disappear in favor of a greater and greater approximation to the model, which the artist seeks to imitate rather than signify."[20] Art ceases to be a social language and becomes a means of individual possession.

The third distinction Lévi-Strauss made between primitive and "civilized" art rested upon the tendency of the latter to develop a self-conscious academicism. Since primitive art is partly collective and unconscious, there is no need for the artist to seek actively to establish himself within a tradition. But in societies like our own artists must constantly attempt to establish ties with the "great masters."[21]

Thus for Lévi-Strauss individualism, representationalism, and academicism were the key factors distinguishing primitive from "civilized" art. The social structure of primitive societies, he argued, militates against the development of these three elements in their art. Since these societies generally consist of a few hundred or a few thousand individuals and generally have less economic stratification than more "civilized" societies, there is less likelihood of a separation between the artist, the artistic public, and the general population. The lives of the individuals in such a society are intertwined, and it is natural that they should share a common set of artistic symbols. This is not the case in a highly "civilized" society, where—to use Lévi-Strauss' own example—a Renault employee virtually never mixes with artists or composers. Art in primitive societies rests upon an all-encompassing network of authentic relationships which do not exist in complex urban civilizations.[22]

In this contrast between primitive and civilized art many of the same sets of oppositions recur that we have already encountered in the description of the seashores, in the typology of landscapes, and in the discussions of European art. But certain themes which are only vaguely outlined elsewhere receive a more thorough statement. Through a series of new oppositions (social unity vs. class divisions, art as an expression of general social, religious, and magical beliefs vs. art as possession of the object, art continued through common, unconscious traditions vs. self-reflective academic art), Lévi-Strauss has come closer to specifying his reactions to the civilization around him. These oppositions serve to define the outlines of two kinds of societies: one in which human beings are bound together by immediate authentic relations; another in which the relations between individuals are distant and mediated through impersonal institutions and ideologies. This contrast adds to the indictment against Western civilization which has been building up throughout all of these passages. Not only has the West lost its ability to mediate between nature and culture and between changeless stagnation and destructive progress; it has also lost the social bonds which bring individuals together into an authentic society. The changes which Lévi-Strauss described in art were only an example of this more general process.

There is one last contrast in Lévi-Strauss' writings which must be examined before the themes first encountered in the passage on Vernet can be placed firmly in their context. Several times in his work, Lévi-Strauss divided human societies into two general types: "hot" societies, such as our own, which are dedicated to rapid change and innovation, and "cold" societies, which seek to remain static. Lévi-Strauss explained the difference between these two kinds of societies by comparing them to machines.

"Cold" societies, he argued, are like mechanisms such as clocks. They begin with a set amount of energy, and they continue to operate at the same level until friction wears them down and some readjustment is necessary. "Hot" societies, by comparison, are more like a steam engine or other thermodynamic machine. These can do far more work than the other mechanisms but they rapidly use up their energy and must be constantly resupplied. Thus "hot" societies are constantly changing and have a visible history, whereas "cold" societies resist change and attempt to continue operating in the same energy-conserving patterns as long as possible.

Moreover, "hot" societies, like thermodynamic machines, draw their energy from differences in potential within the system. They employ internal differences in status and wealth in the form of slavery, serfdom, or class distinctions to create a situation in which the maximum work is performed. Primitive "cold" societies pursue the opposite strategy. Satisfied with relatively low energy levels, they seek to prevent the formation of such internal differences. Many of these societies try to settle all major problems through consensus and may employ ritual combat to exorcise any divisions which appear within the social framework.[23]

Thus Lévi-Strauss conceptualized the differences between "hot" and "cold" societies as a trade-off between power and progress, on the one hand, and harmony and stability, on the other:

> Primitive peoples produce little order through their culture. Today we call them underdeveloped peoples. But they produce very little entropy in their societies. Generally speaking, these societies are equalitarian, mechanical, regulated by the rule of unanimity . . . Civilized peoples, on the other hand, produce a great deal of order in their culture, as is demonstrated by the mechanization and great works of civilization, but they also produce a great deal of entropy in their society: social conflicts, political struggles —all things which, as we have seen, primitives try to prevent, perhaps in a more conscious and systematic fashion than we might have supposed.[24]

This contrast between "hot" thermodynamic societies and "cold" mechanical cultures completes the circle of interlocking metaphors which began with the comments on Vernet. These oppositions may be arranged in a simple chart:

Vernet's 18th century seashore	vs.	The seashore of the twentieth-century
The landscapes of traditional Europe and Latin America	vs.	The exploited regions of Asia and the Americas
Grand classical landscapes	vs.	The restricted subjects of post-Impressionist paintings
Communal and symbolic primitive art	vs.	Private, possessive, and academic Western art
Primitive societies as "cold" and mechanical	vs.	Civilized societies as "hot" thermodynamical machines

If any one of these sets of oppositions had adequately expressed Lévi-Strauss' response to his experiences of Western and non-Western cultures he would probably have simply presented a single contrast and left it at that. But human thought and communication are rarely so simple. It is often necessary to present many partial views of a complex subject in order to point toward that which cannot be fully expressed. Each opposition captures some aspect of Lévi-Strauss' response to his environment—of his being-in-the-world, to borrow a term from the existentialists—but none of them is complete. Therefore, like a musician who develops the same melody in different keys with slight variations in order to produce a more complete musical effect, Lévi-Strauss has presented the same general abstract contrasts again and again, but each time using different concrete terms and altering the pattern slightly. He has transposed the key and changed the melody line a little, but the tune remains quite recognizable.

By reversing this process and moving from the concrete variations to the general pattern of presentation, the historian can begin to develop a clear and communicable theory of Lévi-Strauss' universe. It is necessary to treat each individual description as part of a larger whole and to view the differences between each set of oppositions as transformations within a whole. But once this is done the historian can begin to specify the parameters of Lévi-Strauss' world-view.

Thus Lévi-Strauss' view of society can be seen in terms of two contrasting ideal types which have emerged piecemeal through this analysis. On the one hand there is the world of Vernet, identified with the past, with harmony between man and nature, with slow change, communal property and social organization, lack of class divisions, and a willingness to accept a low level of both power and exploitation. In contrast to this is a type of society in which cooperation between man and nature has been destroyed, in which rapid change and the desire for power have overwhelmed all sense of proportion. It is against this second Faustian world—the world of Western civilization itself—that Lévi-Strauss' polemics are directed.

Such a structural analysis can only perform the first step in a historical investigation. Once this analysis has been performed it is necessary for the historian to return to more traditional methods in order to reintegrate the world-view of Lévi-Strauss into its larger perspective.

But on the basis of this limited analysis it is possible to begin to suggest a new place for the social thought of Lévi-Strauss in modern European intellectual history. Frequently in his writings Lévi-Strauss has expressed his admiration for Marx, and there has been much debate as to whether he can be legitimately considered a Marxist. But this analysis of literary and descriptive passages from his writings indicates that his ideal for society is quite different from the industrialized, cosmopolitan world of the future communist society. Instead his commitment to authentic, unmediated interpersonal relationships, to harmony between man and nature, and to a simple rural life places him more directly in a line of radical thought which passes from Rousseau to the anarchism of Proudhon, Bakunin, and Kropotkin. This hidden affinity for the anarchists was made explicit on one of the rare occasions when Lévi-Strauss allowed himself to comment directly on politics:

> In short [he said in his conversations with Charbonnier], if the anthropologist were to venture to play reformer, to say: 'This is now our experience of thousands of societies can be of service to you, the men of today!' he would no doubt advocate decentralization in all fields, so that the greatest number of social and economic activities could be carried out on the level of authenticity at which the groups are made up of men who have a concrete knowledge of each other.[25]

Thus beneath his pastoral rhetoric Lévi-Strauss may be fulfilling a very different historical role than he himself suspects. He may stand at the end of a tradition of political thought which has been swept away by the world-wide triumph of urban industrialization. He may be the last of the anarchists—a radical who has lost his faith in the revolution.

NOTES

1. Georges Charbonnier, *Entretiens avec Claude Lévi-Strauss* (Paris, 1961), p. 103.
2. Claude Lévi-Strauss, *Tristes Tropiques* (Paris, 1955), p. 391.
3. Ibid., p. 173.
4. Ibid., p. 104.
5. Ibid., p. 105.
6. Ibid.
7. Ibid., p. 144.
8. Ibid.
9. Ibid., p. 145.
10. Ibid., pp. 104-105.
11. Ibid. p. 105.
12. It should be mentioned that Lévi-Strauss' typology of environments could probably be arranged along other axes, although the two given above seem to be particularly important. The four environments could, for example, be viewed in terms of the contrast between the over-populated Indian subcontinent and the underpopulated interior of South America. Once again the traditional countryside is a mediating term, since it has an appropriate population balance. But in this case the exploited areas of the Americas would be closer to the empty interior of South America than to South Asia.
13. Charbonnier, *Entretiens avec Lévi-Strauss*, p. 142.
14. Ibid.
15. Ibid., p. 79.
16. Ibid., p. 143.
17. Ibid., pp. 125-26, 144.
18. Ibid., pp. 63-64, 73-75.
19. Ibid., pp. 75, 88-89.
20. Ibid., p. 66.
21. Ibid., pp. 75-76.
22. Ibid., pp. 109-10.
23. Ibid., pp. 37-46; Claude Lévi-Strauss, *The Scope of Anthropology* (London, 1967), pp. 49-50; *La Pensée sauvage* (Paris, 1962), pp. 309-311. It should be pointed out that in his conversations with Charbonnier Lévi-Strauss cautioned his listeners against applying his comments too literally to all primitive societies.
24. Charbonnier, *Entretiens avec Lévi-Strauss*, p. 45.
25. Ibid., 59.

THE SEARCH FOR THE PRICKLY PLANT: Structure and Function in the Gilgamesh Epic

JOSEPH BLENKINSOPP

THE EPIC POEM ABOUT GILGAMESH, written on twelve stone tablets, was discovered in the British Museum among the more or less twenty-five thousand tablets recovered from the ruins of Nineveh (Kuyunjik) in 1839. In that year a young Englishman, Austin Henry Layard by name, had the good luck to hit on the library of the Assyrian king Ashurbanipal (669-630 B.C.) who cultivated antiquarian interests in time taken out from wars of conquest and devastation. By then stories about Gilgamesh had been in circulation for centuries and some of them had been put together into a cycle or cycles in the Old Babylonian period more than a millenium earlier. Since Layard's day fragments have turned up in several languages and in different places, most recently in Turkey and Israel..

While the standard version found in the library of the Assyrian kings is in Akkadian, the Semitic language spoken in the basin of the Tigris and Euphrates, the basic material of which it was composed was in the language of the Sumerians, a people of unknown origin who settled the alluvial delta-land near the Persian Gulf in the fourth millenium. These "black-headed people," as they called themselves, developed a rich artistic and literary tradition which provided the culture of the Near East with its basic themes and metaphors for centuries. Surviving

Joseph Blenkinsopp, currently Director of Biblical Studies at the University of Notre Dame, taught for some years in England and then at Vanderbilt, Chicago Theological Seminary and Hartford Seminary Foundation. His most recent books are *Gibeon and Israel* (Cambridge, 1972) and *Prophecy and Canon*, to be published next year. Over the last few years he has published several essays in literary criticism of Old Testament material.

fragments of the work of the Babylonian priest-scribe Berossus show that this tradition was still alive as late as the Hellenistic period. At the time of the cultural renaissance of the seventh century B.C. the Sumerian language, which to date has defied classification, was probably about as well known as Latin is in the West today.

I

The subtitle of this paper speaks of the Gilgamesh epic for the simple reason that it has generally been classified as epic. Yet the work itself bears no title nor is its genre specified. In the ancient Near East writings were generally identified by their opening words—this is also the case with the Hebrew Scriptures—and so *Gilgamesh* was referred to as *ša nagba imuru* ("He who saw everything"). This is clearly not very helpful for purposes of classification, nor does it seem that Mesopotamian scribes were much exercised with distinctions of genre. Most of the specialist discussion of the poem (it is at least clear that it is a poem) has dealt with matters pertaining to lexicography, the correct sequence of episodes, the origins of the work, and like questions. As far as I know no one, specialist or student of literature in general, has attempted to examine its structure, and it is conspicuously absent from most discussions of the epic form. It is widely assumed that its central theme has to do with death and that it ends on an unhappy note. Heidel, for example, calls it "a meditation on death in the form of a tragedy" and Henri Frankfort speaks of its "jeering, unhappy, unsatisfactory ending."[1] Yet if typology must follow on morphology such assumptions should not be made before one has examined the structure of the composition.

The point will perhaps emerge more clearly if we agree to start with the assumption that *Gilgamesh* is a myth rather than an epic poem. One of the more obvious characteristics of myths is that they deal with the activities of divine beings and Gilgamesh is, after all, two thirds divine; indeed, if we take in other fragments not in the poem and in the iconography he is divine *tout court*.[2] A distinction between divine and human is complicated by the fact that the boundary between the two realms appears to be quite fluid. The denizens of the one can pass to the other, not all of the divine beings are exempt from death (witness the dream of Enkidu on the seventh tablet), gods rule in the cities of men, and the gradation between human and divine seems to move also on a chronological axis. There are, of course, other ways of defining myth apart from the presence and activity of divine beings. Lévi-Strauss has characterized a myth as a story dealing with events long past which provides a kind of logical tool for resolving contradictions experienced by the group within which the myth operates.[3] He has also evolved a method of considerable ingenuity for exegeting myths and has applied it to a great number of Amerindian myths in the four volumes of his *Mythologiques*. Unfortunately, however, these myths have little in common structurally with *Gilgamesh*—though their themes are sometimes similar—and they clearly came into existence in a quite different way. Thus it would be important to note that several fragments dealing with Gilgamesh and other *dramatis personae* in the poem have come to light and that some of these have been incorporated into it while others have not.[4] This circumstance obliges us to conclude that the genius of the work found in the royal library consisted in the organization of traditional material according to a dominant theme. Hence the question of a shaping intention, quite foreign to Lévi-Strauss' analysis, necessarily arises. In this respect I would agree with Ricoeur's assessment of structural analysis as finding its place somewhere between symbolic naiveté and hermeneutical understanding and his warning that one can pay too high a price for neglecting semantics in favor of snytax.[5]

A further obstacle which stand in the way of an analysis of Gilgamesh in the Lévi-Strauss manner is the historical consciousness within which the work came into existence. We may begin to probe this by noting that Gilgamesh is a king and rules in a real city, Uruk (Warka). In the Sumerian king-lists he is the fifth after the Great Deluge, being preceded by an unnamed king who ruled after the gods once again sent kingship down from heaven, then Enmerkar who built Uruk, then Lugulbanda and Dumuzi. His reign lasted one hundred and twenty years, which, suspicious as it may sound, does not bear comparison with those of the antediluvial kings, which average over thirty thousand years. The action begins with a plan to contain the arbitrary exercise of his royal power and thus leads us to suspect a political intent. Enkidu, who recognized his kingship only after being worsted in a bout of wrestling, may be taken to represent the tribes of the steppe which, as the annals show, were from time to time subdued and brought precariously within the jurisdiction of one or other of the Sumerian city-states. As for Gilgamesh himself, his travels take him through a mythological landscape which is, nevertheless, based on a real if very imperfect and patchy cartography. Thus the Cedar Forest is in Lebanon (an Old Babylonian fragment belonging with tablet V actually gives the name) and beyond it lay the uncharted waters of the Mediterranean. Of Gudea of Lagash, one of the most successful of Sumerian rulers, a cuneiform tablet says that "he made a path into the Cedar Mountain which no man had entered before and cut down the cedars with great axes." He also cut paths through the mountains and mined gold, silver, copper, and precious stones.[6]

Whatever etiological factors may have gone into *Gilgamesh*, it is clear at any rate that it comes from a "hot" society whose scribal tradition laid the bases for Western historiography, with its immediate forebears in Israel and early Christian writers. While this may serve to illustrate Lévi-Strauss' point about writing as an instrument of oppression and control[7] (we recall that *Gilgamesh* was discovered in a library founded by Sargon II, one of the great oppressors of antiquity) it also explains why his method cannot easily be followed here, and also, incidentally, why Leach's application of the same method to biblical material was doomed to failure.[8] The point will be made more forcibly if we go on to suggest that the preoccupation with this dimension of irreversible time leads into the central theme of the work. King Gilgamesh is exemplar of man as achiever and self-creator; he is the anthropological paradigm, the explorer of the outer limits. As he sets out for the Cedar Forest to make a name for himself he reminds us that with kingship the writing of history became possible. The first attempts consist in little more than lists of names with the length of the reign, as in the Sumerian king-lists referred to earlier. Soon, however, it was felt desirable to add short heroic or mythic notes—such as that this king slew a great bear on a hunting expedition or that that one was taken up into heaven by an eagle. If this trajectory is followed we may find a significant clue as to what *Gilgamesh* is about. For we do not need to have recourse to Freud's *Todestrieb* to know that both the making and the writing of history arise out of anxiety about death and constitute an attempt to inflict upon it an at least partial and provisional defeat. The cultural and heroic feats of the hero—the building of city wall and temple, the journeyings, the slayings of monsters—arise out of the anxious knowledge that some day he will die.

II

Before going any further into the question of genre and the discrimination between myth and epic we must try to analyze the work in the form in which it has come down to us. The first and easiest stage is to divide it into its smallest narrative units or "narremes." While there will be occasional uncertainties of order and content, the result will look more or less as follows:

1. G is created by the gods, of superhuman size; he comes to Uruk
2. He rules oppressively there
3. Enkidu is created in the steppe as a counter to G
4. Enkidu oppresses the Trapper and his Father
5. The latter elaborates a plan to transfer Enkidu to Uruk
6. Following the plan, the Harlot is brought from Uruk to seduce Enkidu
7. She does so, and leads him to the city
8. Enkidu meets G, they wrestle and become fast friends
9. G laments not having yet made a name for himself
10. He decides to set out for the Cedar Forest
11. The elders and Enkidu attempt to dissuade him
12. Ninsun his mother and the elders ask Shamash, his tutelary deity, to assist him
13. G consults the omens, which are unfavorable
14. He is equipped with armor and weapons
15. The elders bless and counsel him before departure
16. G and Enkidu travel to the Cedar Forest
17. They encounter the Watchman at the Forest Gate
18. Enkidu opens the Gate with his bare hand; it is paralyzed but then is healed by G
19. G and Enkidu have ambiguous dreams
20. G slays Humbaba the Monster-Guardian and cuts down the Great Cedar
21. Ishtar attemps unsuccessfully to seduce G
22. She forces the high-god Anu to send down the Bull of Heaven
23. The Bull ravages Uruk
24. The Bull is slain by the two Heroes

25. Enkidu throws a side of the carcass at Ishtar, who laments the dead Bull
26. The Heroes return in triumph to Uruk
27. Enkidu has a dream of the Underworld, falls sick and dies
28. G laments Enkidu seven days until a maggot drops from the corpse's nose
29. Afraid of death, G wanders over the steppe
30. He sets out on a journey to find his ancestor Utnapishtim
31. He comes to the Mountain Passes and slays the Guardian-Lions
32. He slays the Scorpion-Man that guards the gate to Mashu the cosmic mountain
33. He passes through the mountain in total darkness
34. He comes into the Garden of Jewels
35. There he meets Shamash and Siduri the vine-goddess, of whom he asks directions
36. Siduri tells him that no one has passed the Waters of Death that lie ahead, but directs him to Urshanabi the Ferryman
37. G destroys the Stone Images used in crossing the water and picks up the magical Urnu-Snakes
38. He and Urshanabi cross the Waters of Death, with the help of one hundred and twenty punting poles
39. He meets Utnapishtim and his Wife and is disappointed
40. Utnapishtim tells him the story of the Great Deluge
41. G fails the ordeal of the week-long vigil by falling asleep
42. He and Urshanabi prepare to depart
43. He is given a last chance: to secure the Prickly Plant at the bottom of the Waters of Death
44. He ties stones to his feet, dives, and secures it
45. On the return journey he loses it to the Snake, which departs sloughing off its skin
46. He returns to Uruk with Urshanabi but without the Plant

We should say that the intentions of a narrative are not always manifested exhaustively in the forward time-movement on its surface. In this case, for example, important clues are to be found in the dreams which, though arranged diachronically, move rather in counterpoint to the shaping intentions of the protagonists. In all except the most pure forms of a story, moreover, there exist elements of tension between the sense or direction of the story in itself (Barthes' *histoire*) and the shaping intention of the storyteller (*discours*). Thus the first column of tablet I reveals the end of the story before it begins—a point not generally noticed. The writer tells us that as a result of his journey through space—which is also a journey backward through time to the days before the Great Deluge[9]—Gilgamesh will obtain wisdom and will thus be in a position to bring back secrets otherwise inaccessible to men. In this way the theme[10] of the Hero as Seeker (or Donative Hero) is announced and, contrary to appearances, his search will be successful *but not in the way he anticipates.* Thus the tension between the *histoire* and the *discours* of the writer introduces a note of irony which is an essential part of the total meaning but which at the same time leaves the story itself intact.

III

If we retrace our steps and begin again with the sequence of actions or functions of which the story is made up our first task will be to see how they are structured. I am therefore proposing to begin by using Vladimir Propp's structural analysis of the folktale[11] and then to compare the results with some standard analyses of the epic. There will of course be other ways but one has to begin somewhere, and this way at least has the advantage of sticking close to the *histoire* of the poem and screening out interpretations of a more general cultural and mytho-theological nature. If we follow Propp we find that after the Initial Situation (1) the story can be divided into three moves. The first (1-8) ends with Enkidu in Uruk. His transference to the city will then lead to the joint adventures of the two heroes (9-26), and this in its turn prepares for Enkidu's death and the ensuing quest of Gilgamesh through space and time for a means of avoiding a like fate (27-46). The justness of this overall division is confirmed by the fact that each of the three moves begins and ends in the city, though the action in each takes place beyond it. The poem as a whole, moreover, begins and ends in the same place with the Hero saying the same words—a stylistic device known as *inclusion*—which invites the question how it is different with Gilgamesh at the end than at the beginning.

The first move begins with a problematic situation (in Propp's terminology, a lack) in the city: Gilgamesh of the restless heart oppresses his subjects. The first stage in the liquidation of this lack is the creation by the Goddess Aruru of the "primitive savage" Enkidu beyond the city walls. His appearance, however, gives rise to another problematic situation, this time in the steppe, since Enkidu sides with the animals against the Trapper. The solution to the situation in both city and steppe is elegantly achieved by the Trapper's Father, who elaborates a plan which will remove Enkidu from the steppe and at the same time counter the restless energy of Gilgamesh. The Mediator will be the Harlot who will come from the city, seduce Enkidu by the watering hole, and lead him, tamed by her sexuality, to the city (6-7). We know, though Enkidu does not, that this is in effect an act of trickery, indeed, an act of divine trickery. For even if the Harlot is not the goddess Ishtar in disguise, the same who will later attempt unsuccessfully to seduce Gilgamesh, still it was the gods' idea to create Enkidu and use him as a counter on their checker-board. Though it remains only implicit throughout, it is of some interest to note that if there is villainy in the story (a central feature in the folktale) it originates in the divine world. Here too there is a sense of tragic irony, which comes to the surface in the description of Enkidu as godlike by both the Harlot and the Citizens of Uruk. For we know that his move to the city will lead unavoidably to his death.

If then we apply Propp's analysis and list the sequence of functions according to his system of notation we have something like the following scheme:

$$\begin{array}{ccc} a^6B^1C & & F^9K^2 \\ & a^6B^1C & \end{array}$$

What this means is that the first move is itself made up of two moves, each beginning with a lack, and both being liquidated by the same means. But the question arises whether Gilgamesh really functions as hero in this first move as he clearly does in the third.

The second move also begins with a deficiency in that Gilgamesh has not yet made a name for himself (9). This can be remedied only by the decision to set out for the Cedar Forest and cut down the Great Cedar guarded by Humbaba, who, we must note, is the appointee of the god Enlil (10). Both here and in the final move Gilgamesh undertakes a journey not just for his own ends but also on behalf of the Citizens of Uruk. There exists therefore in reality a double lack, for we are told that the journey to the Cedar Forest will in some unexplained way remove evil from the land. The Prickly Plant likewise is sought not just for the Hero but for the people in the city. If it were not so, it would be difficult to explain why Gilgamesh, having at long last got his hands on it, did not eat it at once.[12] This corresponds to a basic law of the epic, that in all he does the Hero assumes a vicarious and representative role. In the description of the departure (11-16) we find several of Propp's subsidiary functions: attempts at dissuasion (sometimes by threats and force) and equipping for the journey, in this case with prayers, omens, blessings, and the provision of weapons. There follows the encounter with the unwilling Donor,[13] the Guardian of the Forest Gate who disposes of magic which can only be countered by magic (17). After an initial *faux pas* by Enkidu, who attempts to open the Gate with his bare hands (that is, without the use of magic), the obstacle is at last overcome by the positive reaction of the Hero (18) and they are able to enter the Forest (Propp's Spatial Transference of the Hero). The minatory dreams (19) must be omitted since they move synchronistically with the overt forward movement of the action. The Heroes then engage the Monster in combat, defeat and kill him, and achieve their aim of cutting down the Cedar (20). At this point, however, the liquidation of the lack leads to a further complication in that Gilgamesh's prowess attracts the amorous attentions of Ishtar, prototype of the *femme fatale* in the original and literal sense, the Woman Who Brings Death.[14] This new villainy leads in its turn to a new misfortune, the ravaging of the city by the Bull sent from heaven at her insistence (22-23). This monster from heaven is also despatched (24) and in due course the Heroes return to Uruk in triumph (26). In between, however, the seeds of a new complication have been sown; for as a result of the gratuitous insult of Enkidu, who hurls a part of the carcass at the goddess (25), the gods will take counsel and decide on his death.

In Propp's notation the second move reads as follows:

$$\mathrm{aC}\uparrow \mathrm{D}^9\mathrm{E}^9\mathrm{F}^1\mathrm{G}^2\mathrm{H}^1\mathrm{I}^1\mathrm{K}^1$$
$$\mathrm{aI}^1\downarrow$$

Despite the obvious disproportion, the two sub-moves turn on the same axis of a lack which is removed by a victory; and both take place between the departure from and return to the city.

The impetus for the third and climactic move of the poem comes from the death of Enkidu (27); the message is mediated to

Gilgamesh during the seven-day lament, at the end of which a maggot falls from the nose of the decomposing body (28). After a period of disorientation, typically in the steppe rather than the city, Gilgamesh decides to find a solution to death in the city by seeking out the great ancestor and sage Utnapishtim, also known as Atrahasis, the exceedingly wise one. He therefore sets out once again from the city (30). As in almost all of the hundred tales on which Propp's analysis is based, the hero is tested, interrogated, subjected to ordeals, and attacked before he is able to procure the magical agent. In this instance the "donors" are the Guardian-Lions, the Scorpion-Man, Shamash, Siduri, and Urshanabi the Ferryman (31-37). The decisive obstacle is, of course, the River or Ocean of Death for, like Aeneas, the Hero must cross this great divide before conversing with the ancestor. Despite his destruction of the Stone Images (the identification of which is one of the most vexing problems of the work) he is able at length to cross by magical means (38). This spatial transference between the kingdoms of mortality and immortality brings him at last into the presence of the Great Sage, who, together with his wife, enjoys the *otium cum dignitate* of an immortality achieved by direct grant from the gods (39). After an initial conversation Utnapishtim tells him the story of the Great Deluge and goes on to reinforce the message by subjecting him to an ordeal in which he fails completely (40-41). As he prepared to depart, however (42), a last chance to liquidate the lack is given, but this too is thwarted by the Hero's all too human inattention to the enemy which steals up out of the water (43-45). The life that goes on and on is not, then, for man but for the Snake, which has learned from the earth in which it lives the secret of perpetual self-renewal. And so the Hero returns to Uruk empty-handed, and the story ends as it began with the praise of the architectural glories of the city (46).

This analysis of the third move brings us up against the most obvious characteristic of *Gilgamesh* considered as an epic-biographical work. Several of Propp's functions are again present and in the same order, the action is set in motion by the need for a magical agent, and the subsequent complication is enclosed within the framework of a journey. As nearly as I can see, this gives us the following notation:

$$a^{2}B^{4}\uparrow D^{9}E^{9}G^{4}K^{5}\downarrow$$

The difficulty is, of course, that on this reading the lack is not liquidated, so that it looks at this point more like one of Lévi-Strauss' enigmatic "epics of unavoidable human disaster."[15] It is at any rate fairly clear that while Propp's morphology is helpful for an examination of the individual moves of the poem, especially the first two which pass from disequilibrium to equilibrium, it is less than adequate when used on the poem as a whole. Hence the need to try a different approach.

IV

We may take it that epic deals with great events in the past, that it requires a heroic figure whose exploits it celebrates, and that these exploits generally take place within the context of a journey.[16] We may add, with Paul Goodman, that in epic as opposed to tragedy the action is important in itself rather than as bearing on the character of the protagonist.[17] Yet unlike the folktale (or at least unlike most folktales[18]) the epic can embody a tragic theme, though it is probably going too far to describe the tragic as an essential element in epic.[19] Thus in the *Iliad*, and in *Gilgamesh*, the hero is of divine stock and yet fatally flawed; for it is from his intemperate anger (as from the restless heart of Gilgamesh) that all the evils which follow proceed. A different dimension of the tragic appears in *Beowulf*, which ends with the sacrificial death of the Hero.

The link between the folktale and the epic is to be located in the role of the Hero and the Hero's sphere of action. It is he, in the guise of Seeker, Purifier, or Sacrificial Victim, whose intentions drive the action forward. It would not be surprising, therefore, to find a considerable overlap between Propp's functions and the heroic biography discoverable in the epic. Such a proposition may at any rate be tested, and I propose to do so with the help of some well-known studies of the epic hero-biography. The point of this enquiry (tentative and very preliminary as it will have to be) lies in the structural contrast between these life-histories and the natural cycle of unawakened man, the Solomon Grundy of the old mnemonic rime:

Solomon Grundy
Born on a Monday
Christened on Tuesday
Married on Wednesday
Took ill on Thursday

Worse on Friday
Died on Saturday
Buried on Sunday
This is the end of Solomon Grundy

Over against this "natural" biography we can set, in dramatic or ironic juxtaposition, the life-cycle of the epic hero. Purely for convenience I propose that we conflate the analyses of J. G. von Hahn,[20] Lord Raglan,[21] Jan de Vries,[22] R. Jakobson and M. Szeftel,[23] and finally, in a rather different category, Joseph Campbell.[24] As opposed to the Solomon Grundy pattern of birth, baptism, marriage, sickness, death, and burial the first four of these display, despite considerable variations in detail, the following structure:

Antecedents and Birth	1. Mother a royal virgin (princess) (H,R,V,P 2)[25] 2. Father a god (foreigner, king, near relative of mother, animal) (H,R,V,P 2) 3. Extraordinary, miraculous conception (R,P 3-6) 4. Marvellous birth (born by Caesarian, illegitimate) (H,V,J,P 7) 5. Attempt on life at birth (R) 6. Reaction of nature to marvellous birth (J)
Infancy and Youth	7. Signs of his ascendancy (prophetic discourse) (H,J,P 8) 8. Life threatened (abandoned, spirited away) (H,R,V) 9. Reared by foster-parents (animals, shepherds, mythological beings) in a distant land (H,R,V) 10. Taught reading, writing, occult sciences (J) 11. Manifests special properties (high-spirited, thought to be mad) (H,V,P 13-15) 12. Nothing on his childhood (R)
Struggle and Victory	13. Departure for a distant land (H,R,P 62-70) 14. Preparations for struggle (supernatural help, military equipment) (V,J,P 71-89) 15. Struggle with enemy (dragon, monster, king) (V,J,P 102-5) 16. Victory (H,R,V,J,P 108-9)
Return	17. Triumphant return (H,J,V,P 120) 18. Marriage (R,V,P 151) 19. Slays persecutors at home (frees mother, kills younger brother) (H,V,P 149-50) 20. Becomes king (H,R) 21. Founds cities, makes laws (H,R)

Death	22. Loses favor with the gods (subjects) and is driven out (R) 23. Extraordinary, mysterious death (at young age, by hand of a servant, on top of a hill) (H,R,V) 24. Children do not succeed him (R) 25. Burial in a holy sepulcher (or lies unburied) (R)

It will be seen that Propp's tabulation of the folktale has a somewhat different distribution from that of the epic. It does not, in the first place, enclose the hero-narrative within the framework of birth and death. It gives much greater space to the complication which usually consists in the violation of an interdiction by the victim, leaving him open to a villainy which necessitates the entrance of the hero. This means that the heroic exploit will be introduced at a mature stage of the narrative development (functions 58-60), which in its turn means that the hero's career will not be traced through in a direct and straightforward way. Campbell also omits birth and death, choosing to concentrate on the central *peripeteia* which for him consists in a threefold movement of separation, initiation, and return. Though he does not tabulate functions like the others, he does have them and they may be set out as follows:[26]

Separation	1. The call 2. Departure 3. Supernatural help 4. Defeat of the ogre 5. Crossing of the threshhold
Initiation	6. Tests and ordeals 7. Supernatural help 8. Sacred marriage 9. Atonement for the father 10. Apotheosis or transformation 11. Taking of the elixir
Return	12. Flight by means of magic 13. Rescue from pursuers 14. Crossing of the return threshhold 15. Transformation (resurrection, freedom)

It will be obvious that Campbell has much in common with Propp, though structurally the similarity is blurred by the former's dominant interest in the psychological truth of his scheme. The "dull round" of the birth to death cycle is first broken by a voluntary separation from the familiar world of kinship and the familiar environment of the home. The purpose of this separation is to penetrate to a source of power before reaching which the hero must defeat monsters, undergo the tests and ordeals of initiation, and establish contact with supernatural sources of help. The subsequent crossing of the return threshhold ensures the circulation of spiritual power in the world for which the hero is responsible. It is generally an initial blunder, similar to Propp's violation of an interdiction, which sets the hero on the path of initiation and transfiguration.

It is not to my purpose to embark on a lengthy critique of Campbell's method, though it must be pointed out that he does not provide us with a detailed study of individual heroic narratives as the basis for his conclusions. What he attempted to do was to reformulate the heroic biography according to van Gennep's three stages of initiation rites: separation, transition, incorporation. This procedure must have seemed all the more alluring in that it fitted rather well with a psychological reading of the neo-Pythagorean threefold progression of the soul from *katharsis* through *elampsis* to *henosis*, purification consisting in the trials and ordeals, enlightenment in the rite of initiation itself, and union in the return, more specifically the marriage (though, strangely enough, Campbell puts this last in the second rather than the final stage). On the level of psychological truth we are naturally invited to think of re-union with the mother after overcoming the ogre, the fierce father whose inherited darkness must be transformed into light.[27] The central issue is the necessity of transformation, which must be accomplished here and now, not there and then, in another world, another time.

V

The salient characteristic of Propp's action-analysis is that while the subject is variable the predicate (or function) is constant. In the hero-biography, however, the subject is, by definition, constant while variations occur in the manner in which the life-history unfolds. This does not, of course, imply that for Propp the identity of the *dramatis personae* is of no significance or that in the hero-biography the manner of unfolding is arbitrary and free. In the material on which Propp's analysis is based the perspective is that of the victim of villainy, the one subject to evil, and therefore structurally the principal functions are Lack and Liquidation of Lack. Whether this pattern is more archaic than the heroic biography is an intriguing question which I shall not pursue here—it is probably unanswerable anyway. What has to be noted is that the hero fits into it as mediating between Lack and Liquidation thus creating in effect a triadic pattern: Lack—Mediation—Liquidation of Lack. Common to both types of analysis is that the mediation always involves a departure and return. Whatever else is recorded of him in myth, folktale, or epic, he must undertake a journey from the known to the unknown and back again. This, therefore, has to be regarded as the constant among the numerous variables dealing with birth, early years, complications which occasion the journey, and so on. If then we conflate Prop's analysis with that of the hero-biography as follows:

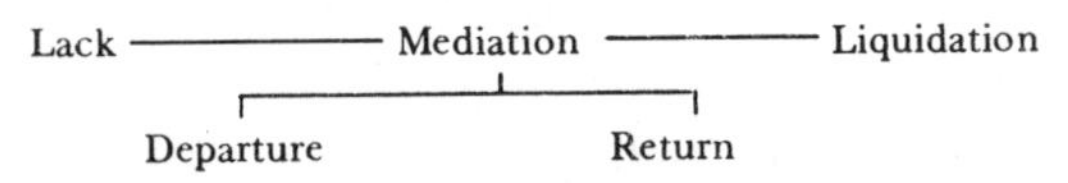

we shall feel justified in drawing the conclusions that the hero-biography is not structurally self-explanatory and, more specifically, that what happens between departure and return must be explained in function of a structure which transcends the hero-biography itself.

To speak of departure/return as a basic structural element, and to identify it as such in *Gilgamesh*, requires first of all that we look at the spatial and temporal co-ordinates of the work and the status of the one who undertakes the journey. We may then be in a position to seek an explanation from outside the work itself without committing ourselves to a functionalist interpretation of it.

We have seen that the city is the point of departure and return in the three moves of the poem. In the first it is set over against the steppe, a spatial antithesis which is well-nigh universal.[28] The city is the locus of the king together with the elders and citizens whom he represents and on whose behalf he acts. Since the city is inseparable from the temple (the earliest Mesopotamian cities were originally temple-communities) it is also the locus of gods; and we have learned that Gilgamesh himself built the temple Eanna for the service of Anu and Ishtar. The steppe, on the other hand, is the place of primitive man, of the subhuman and the animal world; and here it is important to note that Enkidu is described as *lullu*, which is the term for primitive man in the Babylonian creation myth *Enuma elish*. This first spatial antithesis is mediated by the Harlot who passes from city to steppe and returns with Enkidu who is destined to die in the city, that is, out of his natural environment. The paradigmatic nature of this mediation is suggested by the device of trebling: three days during which the Trapper meets Enkidu at the waterhole, three for him to bring the Harlot to the steppe, three for her vigil at the water-hole, twice three for the seduction and presumably three also for the return journey.[29] Here too we have the first correlation between the spatial and temporal axes. We are told that the foundations of Uruk were laid by the antediluvial *apkallu* (the Seven Sages), that the city itself was built by the first postdiluvial king and the city wall and temple by Gilgamesh. The city, therefore, is the point of intersection between space and time, where history is made and recorded and where in consequence death and the anxious knowledge of death are experienced. Enkidu belongs, as we have just seen, to the category of primal man and lives in the timeless and formless world of the subhuman. For him to be brought to the city is to experience, first, the "wisdom" of sexual awakening, then the achieving of great deeds, and finally death, which he attributes to the Harlot.

The existence of protagonists native to these two elements who act in unison for a considerable part of the narrative constitutes an obvious violation of the laws of epic and folk narrative.[30] The only way to explain this anomaly, it seems, is to stress the complementareity of the two principal *dramatis personae*. Gilgamesh, we have seen, is two thirds divine and one third human. In the case of Enkidu the proportions are not specified, but he is clearly more monster than human before his passage from steppe to city. Once this is accomplished the two come together at the center of the range of *dramatis personae*. We may represent it thus:

Subhuman	Human	Superhuman
Monsters	Men	Gods
Immortality	Mortality	Immortality

Enkidu (Immortality–Mortality)   Gilgamesh (Mortality–Immortality)

Unless I am mistaken, we have here a valuable clue to meaning at one level. Man's proper place is in the city, but his situation on the temporal and spatial axis, and especially his relationship with the subhuman and superhuman, leave him open to ambiguity. Gilgamesh of the restless heart covets the immortality of the gods, while Enkidu looks back with regret to the lost world of timeless animality. Together they are the recto and verso of the same human image held together, saved from disintegration, by the tension of centrifugal forces. When Enkidu dies Gilgamesh loses his balance and precarious centredness and the breaking of the tension sends him (so to speak) spinning off to the boundaries of space and time.

To state it with more precise reference to the political and cultural realities which underlie the work, the options which lie before Gilgamesh are: to be a king and consequently to accept mortality and a post-mortem existence in the Underworld and in the memory of posterity; to evade the responsibility of kingship and seek an unending existence beyond the reach of death. In this respect his refusal to be seduced by Ishtar, goddess of Uruk, is in reality a refusal to participate in the city cult, which, here as elsewhere, culminated in the *hieros gamos*. Refusal of death is therefore tantamount to refusal of civic responsibility and threatens the entire structure of the social and political order. Right from the beginning, of course, he knew about death and the acceptable answers to death: the raising of monuments (like the city walls), the making of a name by heroic exploits, and the like. He does not, it is true, ever refer to the hope of immortality through offspring. This is left to Siduri the vine-goddess who, in the most quoted passage in the poem, is not enjoining on him a despairing hedonism—as is almost always assumed—but is simply reminding him of one of the standard answers to death which everyone in the poem except himself seems to acknowledge.[32]

Whereas in the second move Gilgamesh must be accompanied by Enkidu, who knows the way into the regions guarded by monsters (and we may note that Humbaba, like Enkidu himself, has a certain Frankensteinian innocence about him), in the third he sets off alone once the death of Enkidu has led him to his decision. What is the direction, the *sense*, of his movement through space? After an initial period of disorientation in the steppeland he sets off to follow the path of the sun, Shamash his tutelary deity. While his direction, like that of Herakles to the Garden of the Hesperides, is therefore westward, he must also take the sun's path back into the earth as he traverses the tunnel through the cosmic mountain in total darkness. Only in this way can he proceed beyond the furthest point west to reach the "place of sunrise" where Utnapishtim dwells. This direction is not fortuitous, for the sun also, like the ancient earth, knows the secret of dying and rising.[33] But this journey through space is also a journey through time, the time of the great kings and sages before the Deluge with whom alone the wisdom capable of withstanding death is to be found. And therefore, as I have already suggested, the Waters of Death correspond with the waters of the Deluge which he must traverse, as in a film run backwards, in order to have access to the wisdom which sustains life.

We may not be prepared to see the passage through the mountain as a ritual burial and the passage through the Waters of Death as a ritual drowning. It would certainly be hazardous to read the poem against the background of, or in function of, ancient Mesopotamian initiation rites about which we know nothing. But perhaps Campbell, despite his structural imprecision, is right in taking us back to van Gennep's analysis of initiation rites as consisting in separation, liminality, and incorporation, since it at least reminds us that the sense of the journey there and back can be explained only by means of a middle term. We may then at least use such rituals as *analogies* in our attempt to understand the poem without falling into the functionalist trap. We may, for example, note that such rituals (whether of Bushman, shaman, or Christian at baptism) serve for the participants as a kind of pre-mortem death, a way of making death knowable in some way in advance, a way of coming to terms.

What is always of primary importance is the third term, the *nostos* or return home. Like Odysseus visiting the dead Tiresias, Gilgamesh must journey to Utnapishtim at the confines of space and time to find out the way home and to learn to leave the immortality of ego-consciousness to snakes and gods. Hence we are not obliged to conclude with Frankfort, quoted earlier, that the poem comes to "a jeering, unhappy, unsatisfying ending." Gilgamesh had, in Paul Ricoeur's phrase, returned to finitude and learned, not cheaply, about the matter of his death. Like so many ancient compositions it ends as it begins, almost *verbatim*. Gilgamesh is in the same place, saying the same words, *but he is not the same man*. And this is the subtle point that Frankfort misses.

NOTES

1. A. Heidel, *The Gilgamesh Epic and Old Testament Parallels* (Chicago: University of Chicago Press, 1946), p. 10; H. Frankfort *et al.*, *Before Philosophy* (Baltimore: Penguin Books, 1949), p. 227; cf. W. F. Albright, *From the Stone Age to Christianity* (Garden City: Doubleday, 1957), p. 199, who speaks rather imperceptively of its gloomy and hedonistic character.
2. Gilgamesh is listed as a divine name in the Farah Tablets from the Sumerian city of Shuruppak. After his death Gilgamesh becomes lord of the Underworld (see J. B. Pritchard [ed.], *Ancient Near Eastern Texts Relating to the Old Testament* [Princeton: Princeton University Press, 1955], pp. 50-2); and there are other indications that he may have been considered to be a vegetation deity. For the iconography, often of uncertain interpretation, see H. Frankfort, *Cylinder Seals* (London, 1939) [see index], and *Stratified Cylinder Seals from the Diyala Region* (Chicago: University of Chicago Press, 1955), pp. 35ff., 42; and for problems relating to the poem in general, P. Garelli (ed.), *Gilgameš et sa légende* (Paris, 1960).
3. Claude Lévi-Strauss, "The Structural Study of Myth," *Journal of American Folklore* 68 (1955), 428ff.; *Structural Anthropology* (New York: Basic Books, 1963), pp. 206ff.
4. Most obviously, the story of the Great Deluge (tablet XI), existed independently. The myth of Gilgamesh and the Huluppu Tree, or Enkidu in the Underworld, on the twelfth tablet has been shown to be a direct translation from the Sumerian and is also independently attested; see S. N. Kramer, *Sumerian Mythology*, pp. 33-37. Another mythic narrative entitled either *Gilgamesh and Huwawa* or *Gilgamesh in the Land of the Living* stands behind the second move of the composition, for which see Kramer, op.cit., p. 10 and J. B. Pritchard, op.cit., pp. 50-2 (translation by Kramer). Episodes not used are: *Gilgamesh and Agga* (Kramer, p. 40; Pritchard, pp. 44-47) and the *Death of Gilgamesh* (Pritchard, pp. 50-52).
5. "Structure et Hermeneutique," *Esprit*, 31 (1963), 596ff., especially pp. 606ff., 627.
6. Pritchard, op.cit., pp. 268ff.
7. See the remarks of Sanche de Gramont in *Claude Lévi-Strauss: The Anthropologist as Hero*, eds. E. N. and T. Hayes (Cambridge: M.I.T. Press, 1970), p. 14.
8. E. R. Leach, *Genesis as Myth and Other Essays* (London: Jonathan Cape, 1969). What is missing in Leach's studies is consideration of a shaping intention which necessarily involves study of the redactional history of a particular text. In this respect Leach is guilty of the same disregard for the particularity of a "text" with which he charges Lévi-Strauss.
9. He has to go back through time to the antediluvial period and on his journey through space he must cross the Waters of Death, which correspond with this temporal divide. This is also the destiny of Aeneas.
10. For the distinction between theme and motif see V. Propp, *Morphology of the Folktale* (Austin: University of Texas Press, 1968), p. 12.
11. Propp, op.cit., especially Chapter 3, "The Functions of Dramatis Personae."
12. It is likewise difficult to explain why the Man in Genesis 2-3 did not eat of the Tree of Life (nothing prevented him from doing so) without supposing that this ambrosia (= food of immortality) was meant only for consumption in old age. This is one of several respects in which *Gilgamesh* throws valuable light on the biblical "Adamic myth."

13. According to Propp's functions D^8 and D^9 the Donor can be hostile. The term Donor is in these instances admittedly misleading.
14. I have treated this theme as it occurs in Israelite literature (the Davidic Succession History, the Yahwist Work and Proverbs 1-9) in *Supplements to Vetus Testamentum* XV (1966), 44-57.
15. The phrase is Leach's; see his *Claude Lévi-Strauss* (New York: Viking, 1970), p. 83.
16. E.g. *Odyssey, Aeneid, Luciad*. In the *Divina Commedia* and *Pilgrim's Progress* the journey theme is allegorized.
17. "Epics and Epical Actions" in F. H. Candelaria and W. C. Strange (eds.), *Perspectives on Epic* (Boston: Allyn and Bacon, 1965), p. 122.
18. Propp, op.cit., p. 110, allows that there are some few exceptions in which the evil spell is not broken or the hero is not resuscitated.
19. As C. S. Lewis does in "Primary Epic: Techniques and Subject," in A. C. Yu (ed.), *Parnassus Revisited* (Chicago: University of Chicago Press, 1973), pp. 29ff.
20. Johann Georg von Hahn, *Sagenwissenschaftliche Studien*, 1876. I am taking his analysis, based on a study of fourteen "Aryan" heroes, from A. Dundes (ed.), *The Study of Folklore* (Englewood Cliffs: Prentice-Hall, 1965), p. 143.
21. Dundes, op.cit., p. 145.
22. *Heldenlied und Heldensage* (Berne and Munich: Francke Verlag, 1961), pp. 182-89. This work is available in English under the title *Heroic Song and Heroic Legend* (Oxford, 1963).
23. Roman Jakobson and Marc Szeftel, "The Vseslav Epos," in R. Jakobson and E. J. Simmons (eds.), *Russian Epic Studies* (Philadelphia, 1949, pp. 13-52.
24. *The Hero with a Thousand Faces* (Cleveland and New York: Meridian Books, 1956 [first issued 1949]), pp. 245ff.
25. H = von Hahn, R= Lord Raglan, V = de Vries, J = Jakobson and Szeftel; P refers to Propp's functions as set out in Appendix I, Materials for a Tabulation of the Tale.
26. I have based the tabulation on Campbell's detailed description of the hero's progress through the three phases and especially on the summary and diagram on pp. 245ff.
27. Cf. the working out of this theme in the autobiography of Nikos Kazantzakis, *Report to Greco*.
28. For an interesting parallel see Victor Turner, *The Ritual Process* (London, 1969), p. 37.
29. For trebling see Axel Olrik, "Epic Laws of Folk Narrative," in Dundes, op.cit., pp. 132ff. Propp refers to it constantly in his tabulation.
30. See Olrik's laws of "Two in a scene" and "Twins," op.cit., pp. 134ff.
31. We may add that, despite the resulting incongruity, there is more than a suggestion of sexual ambivalence in their relationship. So in his first dream Gilgamesh bends over his friend (symbolized by the star and the ax) as over a woman, and at the end he veils the corpse of Enkidu like a bride.
32. "Gilgamesh, whither rovest thou?/The life thou pursuest thou shalt not find./When the gods created mankind,/Death for mankind they set aside,/Life in their own hands retaining./Thou, Gilgamesh, let full be thy belly,/Make thou merry by day and night./ . . . Pay heed to the little one that holds on to thy hand,/Let thy spouse delight in thy bosom,/For this is the task of [mankind]" (X.iii; Pritchard, op.cit., p. 90).
33. A cylinder seal represents Utu (Shamash) rising out of the earth, and in the iconography in general the sun-god is often associated with chthonic symbols, especially the snake. The scorpion-man, guardian of the mountains of

sunrise and sunset, is also associated with Utu-Shamash. The persisting connection between the sun and the fertility of the earth may be due to the idea that the sun, after setting, passes through the earth and revivifies it. It is of little profit to enquire how Gilgamesh could have been thought to reach the east by passing through the roots of the mountains; but we are not, in any event, obliged to conclude, with John Dunne in *The City of the Gods* (New York, 1965), p. 3 and elsewhere, that he must have been eastbound from the start.

STRUCTURAL NETWORK IN NARRATIVE: The Good Samaritan

DANIEL PATTE

I TURN ON THE RADIO, the room is filled with the announcer's voice. I apprehend the meaning of his text: the President met another chief of state. Indeed, the voice and the meaning seem to be actual entities; yet in both cases I am confronted with an "effect": a sound effect and a *meaning effect*. The sound effect is produced by a series of electronic systems without which I would not hear the speaker and which also impose their constraints upon the sound effect. The structures of the electronic systems allow for the communication of sound and also "filter" it. The electronic systems transmit only part of the sound produced by the speaker and add to it "background noises." Thus in the process of artificial communication a sound is transformed by the interplay of various electronic constraints into a sound effect.

This analogy with all its limitations suggests that, in the process of communication, meaning is communicated as *meaning effect*. Indeed we often have the illusion that meaning is an entity which is the content of a discourse-container. Modern linguistics

Daniel Patte is Associate Professor of New Testament, Vanderbilt University, and director of the interdisciplinary project "Semiology and Exegesis" (a Vanderbilt project sponsored by the National Endowment for the Humanities). He contributes to French and American scholarly journals and is the author of *L'athéisme d'un chrétien ou un chrétien à l'écoute de Sartre* (Paris: N.E.L., 1965), *Early Jewish Hermeneutic in Palestine* (Missoula: Scholars Press, in press), and of *What is Structural Exegesis?* (Philadelphia: Fortress Press, Guides to Biblical Scholarship, in press).

and philosophy have proved that the linguistic expression and the content are inextricably interrelated. A discourse does not *have* meaning; a discourse *is* meaningful. It has a meaning effect, constructed by the interaction of a series of semiotic structures (i.e., the structures of systems of signs).[1] In this statement the term "structure" refers not to the "contour" or "shape" of a meaning effect but rather to the constraints of the systems which produce it.

Semiotics is the study of this complex phenomenon of communication. Semiotic analyses are attempts at "deconstructing" the process through which meaningful discourses are produced—as a sound engineer studies the various electronic components which produce the sound effect that I hear from my radio. Thus, in its first stage, semiotics does not pretend to reveal the meaning of a discourse. On the contrary, the starting point of the analysis is a discourse whose meaning has already been apprehended and is now deconstructed by the analyst. Nevertheless, through this process of deconstruction the analyst becomes aware of components of the meaning effect which otherwise are not consciously apprehended, although they are indeed communicated by the discourse. The total meaning effect of any discourse is only partially apprehended at the conscious level by the receiver—as is clear in the case of poetry which "deeply moves" the reader. In subsequent stages of semiotic research, when the mechanism of the phenomenon of communication begins to be known by the analyst, he can then use this knowledge in an attempt at remedying defective communication of meaning, e.g., when a text is not fully meaningful for the reader.

In the last two decades French structuralists and semioticians (among them C. Brémond, T. Todorov, L. Marin) following the pioneering works of C. Lévi-Strauss, R. Barthes, and A. J. Greimas, have made significant progress toward the elucidation of various components of the phenomenon of communication.[2] The present essay attempts to synthesize the main results of this multifold research by proposing a "model" which shows the interrelation of major semiotic constraints in narrative discourse. This model (or theory) does not pretend to be the only possible representation of the complex phenomenon of communication involved in narrative; it is simply a useful representation (in the same way that the theories about electricity are useful representations).[3] The presentation of such a model (primarily on the basis of Greimas' and Lévi-Strauss' works) presupposes that we have reached the point where it becomes possible to use the first results of fundamental semiotic research in order to remedy some problems of defective communication.

This theoretical presentation is illustrated by an analysis of the parable of the Good Samaritan. This text, like any biblical text, presents problems of interpretation. Because of the cultural distance which separates the modern reader from the biblical text, various aspects of its meaning effect are no longer directly perceived by the reader. I hope to show how a semiotic analysis can help to recover some aspects of the meaning effect.

A meaningful narrative text is produced by means of a *complete* system of human communication—as the sound effect is produced by a complete system of artificial communication (from the microphones in the recording studio to the loudspeakers of my radio). In order to identify the components of this system, we ask the following question: What are the constraints imposed upon narrative texts? The structures which impose their constraint upon such texts can be put into three categories: 1) the cultural structures; 2) the structures of the enunciation; and 3) the deep structures.

I. The Cultural Structures

We are most aware of cultural constraints. Among these we find:

1. The structures of the specific language used in the text. They include not only the superficial syntactic structures of the language but also the structures of this specific system of signs: the paradigmatic structures, that is, the way in which words are phonetically and semantically associated with each other, and also the generative structure in so far as it is characteristic of this specific language.[4] In the text of the parable of the Good Samaritan, as we have it, these structures would be those of koinē Greek. Yet the matter is complicated by the fact that our text is a translation—the original parable was presumably in Aramaic. We have to be aware that we may still have constraints of the Aramaic language at work in our text.

2. The structures which are often termed "cultural codes." They include among others the onomastic, geographical, socio-economic, political, historical, and religious codes. In our text, for instance, "Jerusalem" and "Jericho" belong to the geo-

graphical code; "Jerusalem" also belongs to the religious code (as holy city) together with "priest," "levite," and "Samaritan"; the last three also belong to the socio-economic code, etc. . . .

3. The structures of specific literary styles and genres, in so far as they are characteristic of a given culture. In our text we find the Jewish literary genre *mashal* (approximately, a teaching illustrated by a similitude).

It should be noted that as soon as there is a cultural gap between the author and the reader communication becomes difficult. The reader must learn, or reconstruct, the cultural structures which the author used more or less spontaneously. But, as any historian knows, this reconstruction is never perfect and our knowledge of the cultural structures at work in the biblical texts is necessarily limited; consequently our perception of the meaning effect of these texts is blurred.

Before considering other structural levels let us consider the role of these structures. They impose their constraints upon the discourse. For instance, in order to be meaningful the text must be grammatically correct (both in terms of the surface syntax and of the generative grammar of the specific language) and must satisfy the demands of the cultural codes (the term "robber" cannot directly express the meaning "religious"). Further (and this is less obvious), the literary genre must also be chosen among the genres available to that culture. Thus the structures impose limitations upon the discourse, but this should not be construed as a negative factor since without them the discourse would be meaningless. Without such limitations imposed by the various cultural structures each word has a nearly infinite number of potential semantic connotations (also termed *semantic features* or more technically *semes*) since it can theoretically be defined in terms of all the entries in the dictionary.[5] The superficial syntactic and generative grammars, the codes and the literary genres as structures function as a filtering process which limits drastically the number of connotations for each word. We could say that *the structures select the pertinent semantic connotations, i.e., those which will participate in the meaning effect*.

It should be noted that, despite the filtering function of the cultural structures, there still remains a relatively large number of possible connotations for each word. Traditional historico-literary methods are used in order to study texts in terms of the "cultural structures." But ultimately the scholars have to define each of the key words by constructing complex descriptions of its various possible semantic connotations. In the case of the parable, for instance, the various semantic connotations of many of its key words are described in long articles in the nine-volume *Theological Dictionary of the New Testament*.[6] Thus a large degree of ambiguity remains. If there were only cultural structures at work in a text, the text would be so ambiguous that it would be meaningless. What are the other structures which filter further the potential semantic connotations of the words? We are most aware of other structures which we can term "the structures of the enunciation" and which are also studied by means of the traditional historico-literary methods.

II. The Structures of the Enunciation

These are the constraints imposed upon the discourse by the author and his concrete situation in life. They include:

1. The structure (or logic) of the author's argument. This structure plays an essential role in the semantic filtering process in logical (e.g., philosophical or theological) discourses. In stories, in poetry, and in mythological texts, however, this kind of logical structure is almost totally absent and has a minimal role in the filtering process. This is the case with the parable of the Good Samaritan (Luke 10:30-35). We can note, nevertheless, a mark of the author even in such texts: the specific style. In the case of our text Jesus reduced the Jewish literary genre *mashal* to the subgenre "parable." Here the interaction of two structures (the cultural structure of the "literary genre" and a structure of the enunciation) results in a more specific literary genre which is especially adequate for the production of a specific type of meaning effects—the meaning effects which characterize Jesus' teaching. The semantic filtering process is therefore reinforced.

2. The constraints of the concrete situation in which the discourse is uttered, including:

a. The place of the discourse in the broader argument of the author. We know the place of the parable in the gospel writer's argument (how he understood Jesus' parable, cf. Luke 10:25-37) but we do not know its place in the historical Jesus' teaching.

b. The situations in life (*Sitze im Leben*) and their impact upon the author. We do not know in which specific situation Jesus taught this parable: if it was in a polemic against the priests and levites, the parable would have a meaning effect which it would not have in another situation. Luke provides a situation for the parable itself, but what was the specific situation of the early Hellenistic church in which this interpretation of the parable was proposed?

Even when there is no cultural gap and when all the structures of the enunciation are known, the two preceding structural levels are not sufficient to explain the complete meaning effect of a discourse. There are structures which are so omnipresent that they are often not noticed and which, when noticed, are considered, because of their universality, irrelevant for the elucidation of the meaning effect. It might indeed be so when there is no problem of communication (i.e., when the structures of the other two levels are apprehended by the reader, and thus function also for the reader). But in the case of defective communication, as we shall see, knowledge of the universal structures is most useful. These structures are those which the structuralists study—thus structuralism has to be viewed as a subdiscipline of the more general field of semiotics. We term these structures "deep structures."

III. The Deep Structures

These structures are said to be "structures of the human mind," "symbolic functions of the human mind" (Lévi-Strauss), or "innate structures" (Chomsky). We may want to refer to them as "archetypal structures." Without entering the philosophical debate about their ontological status,[7] we can simply say that these deep structures are constraints imposed upon any discourse and that they participate in the semantic filtering process suggested above. As "filters" they are semantically empty (thus they should not be equated with Platonic ideas).

Models for the deep structures have been established on the basis of analyses aimed at identifying the constants in various aspects of the phenomenon of human communication. These constants are not phonetic features or semantic features—also termed features of the expression and of the content, respectively—but are rather specific *relations* which link these features together. These constant relations can be viewed as forming several "networks of relations" or "structures" which interact with each other. Because of their relational nature, these structures can be represented only by means of abstract models or algebra-like formulae.

Because we are concerned with the study of *meaning* effects we shall limit our discussion in this essay to deep structures of the content, yet it should be kept in mind that the deep structures of the expression (e.g., the deep phonetic structures) are usually viewed as isomorphous with the deep structures of the content and as such have provided models for the study of the latter. We shall deal with three deep structures of the content: the narrative structure, the mythical structure, and the elementary structure. We shall suggest how these three are interrelated so as to form a complex filtering process.

A. *The Narrative Structure*[8]

In order to avoid any misunderstanding, it might be useful to state again what we mean by the term "structure." It is not the contour or shape of the narrative text but rather the constraints which preside over the production of a meaningful narrative text. It is the relational network which is presupposed by the author as well as the reader and demands that the semantic features be interrelated in specific ways to produce a narrative meaning effect. Using again the metaphor of filtering, we could say that the narrative structure is performing an additional filtering of the semantic features which have already been selected by the filtering process of the other structural levels. Because of the limited number of semantic features remaining, we can expect that only parts of the new "filter" will be used in each specific case. In other words, each narrative text manifests only a part of the narrative structure even though the whole structure is presupposed.[9] For simplicity's sake we shall describe the narrative structure in terms of the presuppositions we have when reading a narrative. Yet it should be kept in mind that the model has been established quite differently—by comparing large numbers of narrative texts in order to distinguish constants from variables. As we proceed we shall introduce the main technical vocabulary used by Greimas and his followers.

1. *The Narrative Functions*. "A man was going down from Jerusalem to Jericho." A personage is doing something. This is an action, more specifically, a movement which includes a *disjunction* (he left Jerusalem) and a potential *conjunction* (he hopefully will reach Jericho). This action, like any action, is implicitly related to other actions. We indeed spontaneously presuppose that there is some purpose to this journey: in Jericho

this man would do something. He would perform some kind of task. For instance (and this is a totally arbitrary hypothesis), he would go to a potter's and buy a pot for a friend. In fact, we presuppose three types of performance: *confrontation*—he would meet or confront somebody or some situation (the potter with pots); *domination or submission*—he would deal successfully or not with this person or situation (buying nor not buying the pot); *attribution*—if successful, he would give the pot to the friend.

We also presuppose that the man decided to make this journey and to perform this task: for instance, his wife asked him to do so and he accepted this *mandate*. This acceptance implies that he has the will (or *volition*) to carry out this task. But in order to do so he needs to know where the potter lives, and to have the means (or *power*) to carry out this task—for instance, he needs money and physical strength. We presuppose therefore the *communication* of *cognition* and *power* to the personage (this communication might have taken place before the mandating).

We could make many other presuppositions but the above "actions" are the only ones which have been found to be constants in any narrative. This series of "actions" which is a major component of the narrative structure can be termed *narrative sequence*. Since we are dealing with an abstract structure (a relational network), what we have called "actions" should be designated *functions* (a relational term). Thus a narrative sequence includes the following *functions: mandating* (establishment of the volition), *communication* (of cognition and power), *disjunction/conjunction* (the movement necessary to perform the mandate), *confrontation, domination/submission*, and *attribution*.

Two remarks are needed here. First, the narrative sequence can be interrupted at any point. In the case of the parable, the sequence of the man's "actions" is interrupted at the level of the function disjunction/conjunction: his journey is interrupted. Second, the function "disjunction" is the only one manifested in our particular text: the semantic filtering by a structure of the enunciation (the author's intention) has dismissed as not pertinent any mention of the man's purpose and has disallowed the manifestation of all but one function. Our story of the man's hypothetical visit to the potter does not belong to this text. We know only that "a man was going down from Jerusalem to Jericho."

2. *The Actantial Positions*. Each function puts in a specific relation several narrative semantic features (most often personages or actors). In other words, each function can be viewed as a micro-relational network which includes, as Greimas pointed out, six positions. A narrative semantic feature (e.g., an actor) is pertinent only if it occupies one of these six positions (called *actantial positions* or *actants*) and is in this way put in relation with the semantic features (e.g., other actors) of the other five positions. We shall use our hypothetical reconstruction of the man's story to bring some concreteness to our discussion.

The function *mandating* interrelates several narrative components: the wife, the pot, the friend, and the man. The wife would like to give a pot to a friend. This is manifestation of three interrelated actantial positions that we can transcribe more abstractly as follows: the *sender* wants to transmit the *object* to the *receiver*. In order to do so the sender (the wife) gives to somebody (the man) the mandate to perform the actions required to transmit the object to the receiver. Thus a fourth actantial position is manifested in our story: the man is in the actantial position of *subject*.[10] The mandate also presupposes that there is some kind of obstacle to the transmission of the object. The obstacle is manifested by the actantial position of *opponent* (say, by the cost of the pot). This fifth actantial position implies a sixth one: the subject will need the necessary helpers in order to overcome the opponent(s). This actantial position is simply termed the *helper* (manifested in our example by the money).

This micro-relational network of any function can be represented in the following *actantial model* (the arrows express the main relations):

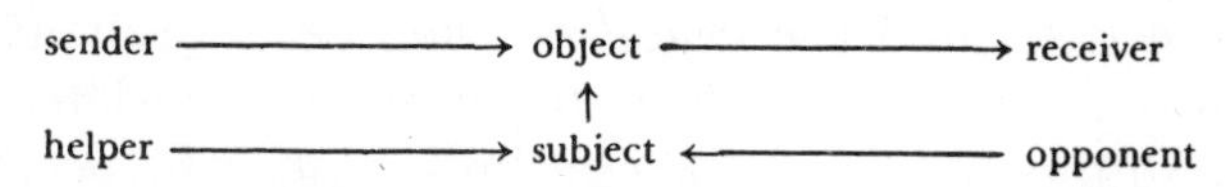

Each function emphasizes particular actantial positions even though it presupposes the entire actantial model. *Mandating* emphasizes the positions of the subject, object, receiver, and often sender; *communication* the helper and thus indirectly the opponent; *confrontation* the opponent and the helper (the subject sizes up the opponent); *domination/submission* the helper, subject, and opponent (either the subject and his helpers dominate the opponent or submit to him); *attribution* the subject, object, and receiver (the subject transmits the object to the receiver).

For each function in a given sequence the manifestation of the actantial model is basically the same, with the exception of the positions of helper and opponent: new opponents might appear at any point in the sequence (e.g., the robbers in the parable) and create the need for new helpers.

3. *The Narrative Structure as a Whole*. The narrative structure can be viewed as a network of narrative sequences interrelated in specific ways. We can distinguish three types of sequences according to their role in the narrative structure: correlated sequences, topical sequences, and sub-sequences.

A structural reading of any narrative presupposes that there is a need to transform an initial situation: there is a *lack* which must be overcome. The initial situation, then, is a sequence which has been interrupted in one way or another—often by the subject's being deprived of his helpers. The narrative itself consists of attempt(s) (expressed by one or several sequences) to reestablish the possibility of carrying out the initial sequence so as to lead eventually to a final sequence and completion or balance. The initial and final sequences are thus *correlated*: they are the beginning and end of the same sequence. In the parable we are considering, the initial sequence is manifested by the story of a man whose journey is interrupted by robbers. He is in a situation of lack, deprived of his belongings and of his vigor or strength (both are his helpers).[11] The final sequence is manifested *not* in this particular text but through our acquaintance with other texts we presuppose it: we hope that eventually the man's good health and belongings will be restored to him and that he will be able to carry out his business in Jericho.

The sequence which expresses how the lack is (eventually) overcome is termed the *topical sequence* because of its central place in the narrative. Somebody receives a mandate to act to reestablish the initial sequence; if he accepts it he becomes the subject of the topical sequence, or the hero (the sender who proposes this mandate may or may not be manifested). In the topical sequence in this parable the Samaritan discovers the lack (the wounded man). A mandate is implied in this discovery: by showing him the lack, an unknown sender (chance? God?) suggests a performance. He accepts this mandate (he has compassion) and does all that he can to overcome the lack. For this purpose he uses several helpers—know-how, oil, wine, donkey, money, innkeeper. (Let us note that two other topical sequences have aborted: the same mandate was proposed to the priest and the levite and both refused it.)

One or more instances of a third type of sequence are usually found in narrative texts: the sub-sequences. These complement the correlated and topical sequences by telling a story about one of the actors in order to explain what happens in the main sequences.[12] The story of the robbers in our parable is a sub-sequence which describes the opponents who created the lack in the initial correlated sequence. Similarly we could imagine a more detailed sub-sequence describing the innkeeper who is one of the helpers in the topical sequence and also a sub-sequence describing what the Samaritan was doing before seeing the wounded man.[13] In more complex narratives the sub-sequences can evolve into complete sub-narratives.

The narrative structure includes a potentially infinite number of sequences. In the analysis of complex narratives the most delicate task is the elucidation of the structural hierarchy of the sequences: the order of the text does not necessarily suggest it. This hierarchy is essential to the analysis because it determines the semantic value of each of the narrative features. For instance, the sub-sequence of the robbers defines the opponents of the man and consequently defines the semantic value of the man himself.

B. *The Mythic Structure*

1. *Progressive Mediation of a Fundamental Opposition*. The narrative structure as it has been outlined here is most evidently at work in narrative texts, yet it is also at work in subtle ways in other types of discourse (in liturgies, in logical discourses, etc.); there are many kinds of "objects" which can be transmitted. If indeed this narrative structure is one of the archetypal structures, any human perception and expression of reality is filtered by it. Similarly the mythic structure is most evidently at work in mythological texts but is not limited to them. We can easily understand that it might be at work in non-mythological religious texts[14]—e.g., in Jesus' parables—yet it is also at work in subtle ways in any human communication. As opposed to the narrative structure, which seems to allow for the apprehension of reality as a meaningful process, the mythic structure seems to allow for the apprehension of reality as a meaningful system of reference.

Lévi-Strauss suggested a model for mythic structure, demonstrating it by the analysis of more than eight hundred myths.[15] Mythic structure, as an archetypal structure, imposes upon man a perception of reality in terms of binary oppositions of complex semantic units that Lévi-Strauss called *mythemes*.[16] The mythical structure as a relational network organizes these oppositions in a hierarchical fashion: a fundamental opposition which does not admit of direct mediation (e.g., life/death) is considered as equivalent to an opposition which admits of a mediation; this second opposition is considered as equivalent to a third one which admits of an easier mediation, and so on. Let us illustrate our discussion by making use of a few elements of Lévi-Strauss' analysis of a Zuñi myth.[17] Life and death is a fundamental opposition which cannot be directly mediated. It is symbolically viewed as equivalent to the opposition "agriculture" (life-giving) vs. "warfare" (bringing death). This second opposition admits a mediating term: hunting. Like agriculture, hunting provides food; like warfare, hunting involves killing. A third opposition is developed out of the second: animals which hunt (i.e., predators) can be viewed as equivalent to warfare, and herbivorous animals to agriculture. This opposition has an obvious mediating term: the scavenger, which eats flesh like the predator and yet like the herbivore does not kill. This brief series of oppositions (which is only a small part of the mythical structure in all the Zuñi texts) provides therefore a progressive mediation of the fundamental opposition which taken in itself does not admit of a mediation and confronts man with an existential dilemma. The mythical structure unites as a meaningful universe a potentially meaningless and broken existential reality. In the case of this version of the Zuñi myth, death is viewed as sustaining life. Lévi-Strauss represents the mythical structure in this text as follows:[18]

Life		
	Agriculture	
		Herbivore
		Scavenger
	Hunting	Predator
	Warfare	
Death		

2. *The Pertinent Semantic Features Selected by the Mythical Structure*. The mythical structure selects two semantic features

(or semes) as the only pertinent ones (i.e., as the only ones which participate in the meaning effect) for each of the terms of the opposition. The mediating terms perform their mediating role because (and only because) they have one semantic feature in common with each of the two poles of the opposition they mediate. "Killing"[19] is the semantic feature common to both "warfare" and "hunting"; "food" is the semantic feature common to both "agriculture" and "hunting." (Note that "killing" is a function—an action—and "food" a state—a thing.) In the second pair of oppositions the term "hunting" has the same pertinent semantic features ("killing" and "food") even though it is now symbolized by "predator." Since any pole of any opposition can potentially be the mediating term of another opposition, any term has two pertinent semantic features: a function and a state. We can now represent more abstractly the opposition "warfare/hunting/agriculture" in the following algebra-like formulation in which "x" and "y" represent functions and "a" and "b" states.

$F_y(b)$	Agriculture
$F_x(b)$	Hunting
$F_x(a)$	Warfare

On the basis of the preceding remarks we can say that the semantic features "x" and "b" are respectively "killing" and "food."

As Lévi-Strauss has shown, the mythic structure also imposes very specific constraints upon the relation of two oppositions. As we have seen, one of the poles (hunting) of the second pair of oppositions is made out of the semantic features of the preceding opposition since this pole ($F_x(b)$) is also the mediating term of the preceding opposition. What about the polar opposite of $F_x(b)$? If the predator is $F_x(b)$, what is the formula for the herbivore in this myth? Lévi-Strauss has shown that it is also defined by the semantic features found in the preceding opposition. In order to understand this we need to analyze further the Zuñi myth and determine tentatively the semantic features represented by "y" and "a."[20]

Warfare is killing enemies. Thus "a" is "enemies" (a state). Agriculture is "gathering" food. Thus "y" is "gathering" (a function). What is a herbivore? It is primarily an animal which can be "gathered" as food. In other words, the *function* "y" ("gathering") is present in the herbivore as a *state* "y" ("gathered"). A herbivore is also a friendly animal, an animal which neither attacks man nor acts as an enemy. Thus the *state* "a" ("enemies") is also present in herbivore as a *function* in a *negative* form ("$\bar{a}$"). Thus the herbivore can be represented as $F_{\bar{a}}(y)$. This formulation of the second pole of the second pair of oppositions was found by Lévi-Strauss to be a constant and not a variable. Thus he could formulate the relation of two pairs of consecutive oppositions in the mythical structure as follows:

$$F_x(a) : F_y(b) :: F_x(b) : F_{\bar{a}}(y)$$

This formula can be read, in terms of the Zuñi myth, warfare is to agriculture as predators are to herbivores.

3. *Mythic Structure and Narrative Structure*. These two structures filter the semantic features in two quite different ways. While the narrative structure selects the semantic features which produce a meaningful *process*, the mythic structure selects those which produce a meaningful *system* of reference or, in traditional cultures, a meaningful *religious* system. Nevertheless they do not function independently from each other, as is demonstrated by the fact that myths are also narratives. We can envision their interrelation as the intersection of the mythic and narrative planes. It appears that the personages of the narrative which are defined by their actantial positions and their narrative functions in various sequences also function as terms in the mythic oppositions. A given narrative usually defines only one mythic opposition and its mediation and merely alludes to the preceding opposition which it mediates.[21]

What are the narrative elements which could be viewed as the opposing terms of the mythic structure? Some have proposed that they are the contents of the two correlated sequences—the situation of lack and the situation of non-lack—the mediating term being the content of the topical sequence.[22] This *cannot* be the case, for it in effect reduces the mythic structure to the narrative structure and thereby confuses two logically distinct categories. The oppositions of the mythic structure are oppositions of *contraries* comparable to the opposition "life vs. death" (or "God vs. man"). The opposition "lack vs. non-lack" would be comparable to the opposition "life vs. non-life" (an opposition of *contradictories*).[23] I would like to propose that the *situation of lack* which is indeed an essential semantic unit in the narrative should rather be opposed to the *semantic value of the hero*, that is, the subject of the topical sequence as defined by his relation to the other actantial positions (and especially that of helper) and the functions he performs. The situation of non-lack (lack overcome) is the mediating term. Furthermore, the hero appears to function as the mediating term of the preceding opposition. Thus the hero is the pole $F_x(b)$, and the situation of lack the pole $F_{\bar{a}}(y)$. (I believe this to be a constant, that is, a part of the deep structure which governs the relationship between mythic and narrative structures. This part of the structural model is being verified by the analysis of as many texts as possible).

We have therefore the following manifestation of the mythic structure in the parable of the Good Samaritan:

$F_y(b)$	
?	$F_{\bar{a}}(y)$
	wounded man
	healed man
$F_x(b)$	$F_x(b)$
Samaritan	Samaritan
$F_x(a)$	
?	

What is the opposition that precedes those that appear here? I suggested that the narrative *alludes* to it because there does not seem to be any rule pre-selecting narrative elements for these terms. However, by an analysis of the semantic value of "Samaritan" and "wounded man" as defined by the narrative as a whole (and *not* as defined by the cultural codes), we should be able to identify the semantic features represented by "x," "y," "a," and "b" and then to identify $F_x(a)$ and $F_y(b)$. In so doing we are dealing no longer with complex semantic units (the polar oppositions) but with elementary semantic features. At that level we find the constraints of another deep structure: the elementary structure.

C. *The Elementary Structure*

The structure often called the semiotic square is nothing other than Aristotle's logical square. Any semantic feature has both a contrary and a contradictory: life has the contrary death and the contradictory non-life (e.g., non-living matter). There is also a relation of implication between the contrary and the contradictory: thus death implies non-life. If we consider the opposition in terms of the other pole of the opposition of contraries—death—we find that it has also a contradictory—death has as its contradictory non-death—and we find another relation of implication—life implies non-death. Thus we have the square:

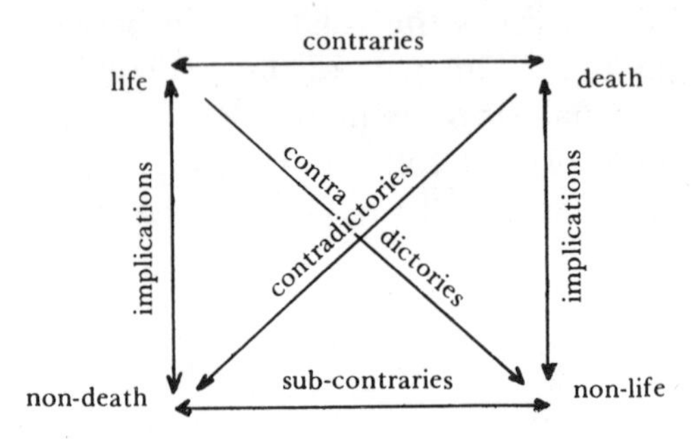

1. *Elementary Structure and Mythical Structure*. Since the opposition $F_x(a)$ vs. $F_y(b)$ is an opposition of contraries, we can deduce that x vs. y and a vs. b are also oppositions of contraries.

We have therefore two squares: the square of the functions and that of the states.

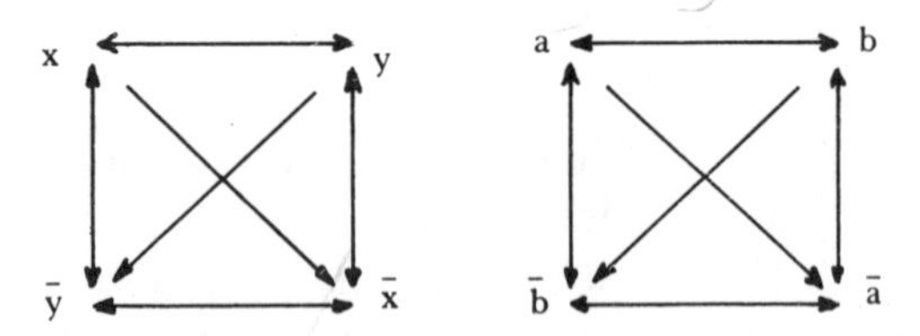

Let us emphasize the relation of implication: x implies $\bar{y}$, a implies $\bar{b}$, etc. . . . In the pair of polar terms, as they are defined through the complex interaction of the narrative and mythic structures, we can expect to find the complete square, with all of the relations of each semantic feature.

2. *Semantic Analysis of the Parable (Part I)*. Let us first consider the semantic value of the function x and of its implications $\bar{y}$ (i.e., the function of the term "Samaritan"). We find that he is compassionate, he approaches a wounded person, he helps, he gives money (to the innkeeper). The contrary attitudes (y and its implication $\bar{x}$) appear clearly: there are people without feeling (robbers, priest, and levite) who leave, abandon, pass by without

being compassionate, without approaching the wounded man, without helping. There are also people who take violently and rob (the robbers). Their actions are contraries to giving money and being honest. These remarks about y and $\bar{x}$ show how to divide the various semantic features between the opposition of contraries and that of sub-contraries. We can now manifest the square with these functions.

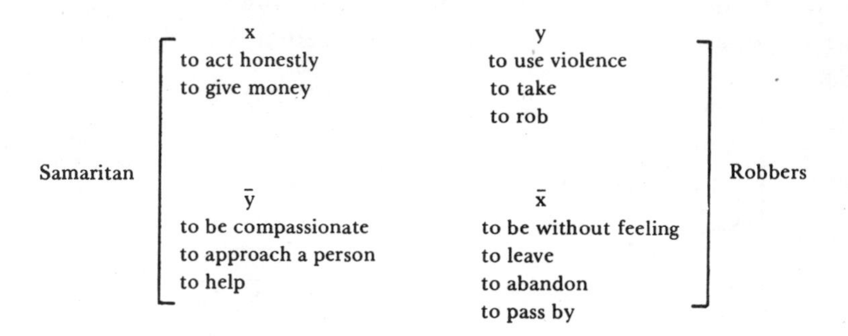

"y" (and its implication $\bar{x}$) clearly characterize the robbers. The wounded man manifests the term $F_{\bar{a}}(y)$. The state y (the result of the action y) is the result of violence, the state of being wounded and deprived of one's belongings. The priest and levite manifest $\bar{x}$ but not y.

Considering now the states, we should begin with b and its implication ā, semantic features which we know characterize the Samaritan and should also characterize the robbers, if our preceding analysis is correct. But what have they in common in the text? Let us not forget that ā is also a function in $F\bar{a}(y)$. What is the function of the wounded man? The only clue the text gives us is that he is on the roadside, in the ditch. What could ā be as a state? Not on the road? What then could be a? To be on the road? Looking at the text more closely, we discover that it expresses the direction in which the man, the priest, and the levite are going. The man was "going down from Jerusalem to Jericho"; the priest "was going down that road." Of the levite it is said "*So likewise* a levite, when he came to the place," implying a directed travel in terms of ordered space. By contrast, the Samaritan is "journeying": the verb does not suggest any direction. We do not know which way he is going; his journey is not spatially ordered. The same is true of the robbers: we do not know from which direction they have come or where they are going.

This is all that is manifested in the narrative about the states. This should not surprise us: a narrative primarily describes processes and functions, while the states are qualifications, sometimes expressed in description. The narrative structure does not emphasize the states clearly enough and the mythic structure is no help in the analysis at this point. We shall have to call upon other structural levels.

Let us nevertheless summarize what we have found by constructing a square of states, which still remains incomplete:

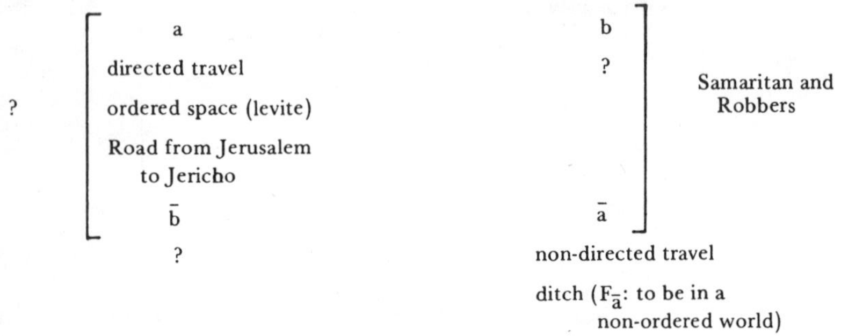

?

a
directed travel
ordered space (levite)
Road from Jerusalem
to Jericho

b
?

Samaritan and
Robbers

$\bar{b}$
?

$\bar{a}$
non-directed travel
ditch ($F_{\bar{a}}$: to be in a
non-ordered world)

3. *Semantic Analysis of the Parable (Part II)*. In order to complete this analysis and to reconstruct the religious meaning effect of this parable we need now to call upon the cultural codes. As we noted in the beginning of this discussion, we have a very imprecise knowledge of these codes because of the cultural gap which separates us from this text. Yet because of our awareness of the filtering process of the deep structures we can easily identify the pertinent semantic features which were used to produce the meaning effect.

What is "b"? What state is common to a robber and a Samaritan? They are both rejected by religious people: a robber was irreligious—or better, a-religious; in mythological terms, he was a symbol of chaos. A Samaritan was a heretic, but he was also a symbol of chaos for the Jews of that time, because Samaritans had profaned the Temple in Jerusalem. That these are indeed the semantic features which manifest b is confirmed by the relation of implication: in mythological terms chaos (b) implies a non-ordered world and thus non-directed travel. (The inn also appears as a figure of this non-ordered world.)

What is $\bar{b}$? "a" expresses the directed travel of the man, priest, and levite. According to the cultural codes the priest and levite are clearly religious personages: "$\bar{b}$" is therefore "religious," in mythological terms non-chaotic. The deep structure suggests that the man is also a religious Jew. Among the many potential semantic features that the word "Jerusalem" could have according to the cultural codes only two are retained: Jerusalem as geographical location which orients travel (as Jericho does) and Jerusalem as symbol of "religion" or more specifically of the Jewish religion. We can now present a more completely manifested square of states:

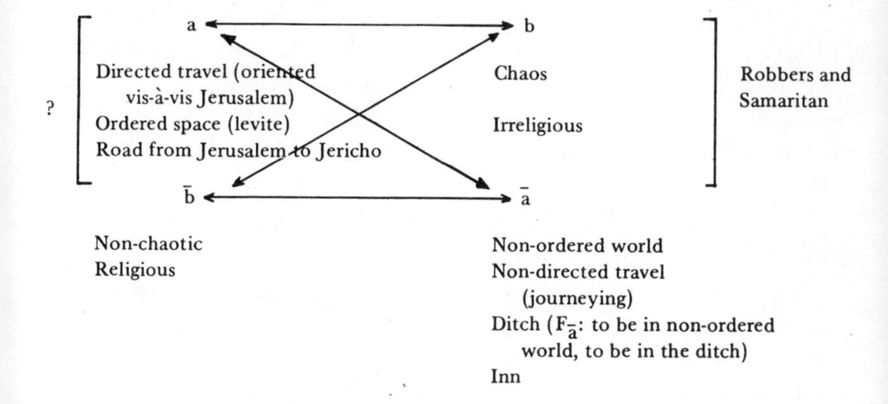

IV. Results of the Structural Analysis

We can now go back to the mythic structure. What is the semantic value of the mytheme $F_x(a)$? The characteristics of x and $\bar{y}$ and of a and $\bar{b}$ are not manifested in any single personage of the text. The semantic features a, $\bar{b}$, and x are manifested in the personages of the priest and levite. But they do not possess the feature $\bar{y}$; rather they possess its contrary $\bar{x}$. $F_x(a)$ is therefore an ideal, a truly Jewish religious person. From what we know about Jesus' teaching we could dare to say that the term represents a person who belongs to the Kingdom. The mythical structure reads now:

Robbers	wounded man
ideal religious person	Samaritan

That is: the truly religious person is to the robbers as the Samaritan is to the wounded man. The Samaritan is symbolically identified with the truly religious person in the same way that the wounded man is symbolically identified with the robbers (irreligious people).

The Samaritan is symbolically identified with the truly religious person because he provides a valid mediation between him and the robbers (chaos). The priest and levite fail to provide such a mediation—even though according to the cultural codes they are expected to do so. The semantic difference is clear: the Samaritan *acts* as the truly religious person would (the semantic value x and its implication $\bar{y}$) and has the same *state* as the robbers (b and $\bar{a}$: he is in a chaotic, non-ordered world) and therefore does not have the privileged *state* that the truly religious man has (a and $\bar{b}$: a religiously ordered world, ideally, a state like paradise). By contrast the priest and levite have the *state* of the truly religious person (a and $\bar{b}$) and *act* partly as the robbers do ($\bar{x}$).

The semantic effect of the parable deeply challenges the traditionally religious: as long as they do not venture outside of their religiously ordered world and become irreligious, they cannot be symbolically identified with the truly religious person—they do not belong to the Kingdom—and consequently they cannot act like the truly religious person. As long as they remain priest and levite (and Jew) they cannot help the wounded man in the ditch. This text does not propose an example which the reader could directly and readily duplicate in his own life. It is not a matter of *acting* as the Samaritan did, but of *becoming* like a Samaritan. Thus, the analysis excludes the possibility that this text is an example story, as many interpreters have proposed.[24] This misinterpretation began with Luke himself: according to him Jesus exhorted the lawyer to "go and do likewise" (Luke 10:37). Because of the cultural gap which separated the Hellenistic Luke from the Palestinian Jesus, the challenging character of the parable was dismissed; the parable became an example story. A structural analysis of Luke 10:25-37 (i.e., Luke's story of the dialogue between Jesus and a lawyer) would allow us to apprehend the meaning effect of Luke's text, as opposed to Jesus' parable.

NOTES

1. The fundamental theoretical tenets on which the structural analysis of text is based, have been established by A. J. Greimas in his books, *Sémantique structurale. Recherche de méthode* (Paris: Larousse, 1966); *Du Sens. Essais sémiotiques* (Paris: Seuil, 1970). In English see A. J. Greimas, "Narrative Grammar: Units and Levels," *Modern Language Notes* 86 (1971), 793-806; and A. J. Greimas & F. Rastier, "The Interaction of Semiotic Constraints," *Yale French Studies* 41 (1969), 86-105.
2. For a minimal bibliography on these authors see J. D. Crossan, "A Basic Bibliography for Parables Research," *Semeia* (Missoula: The Scholar's Press, Society of Biblical Literature), 1 (1974), 264-66.
3. As in the natural sciences (e.g., nuclear physics), the presentation of a model (or theory) always implies the opening statement: "According to the present stage of research, it is as if . . ." For instance, "it is as if there are electric waves . . ." or "as if there is a flow of electrically charged particules." For the scientist making this statement these are presently the most adequate representations of the phenomenon. Thus we simply affirm: according to the state of specific research on the phenomenon of communication it is as if there is a network of structural constraints which produces meaning effects. On the notion of model in science see Ian G. Barbour, *Science and Secularity: The Ethics of Technology* (New York: Harper & Row, 1970), pp. 10-31.
4. As we shall see below there are dimensions of the generative grammar as studied by N. Chomsky which belong to the level of deep structures.
5. Professor W. von Raffler Engle, Professor of Linguistics at Vanderbilt University, called my attention to this important result of componential analysis. The polysemic nature of words is also discussed in the essay by Paul Ricoeur, "What is a Text?" in D. M. Rasmussen, *Mythic-Symbolic Language and Philosophical Anthropology* (Martinus Nijhoff: The Hague, 1971), 135-50.
6. G. Kittel ed., *Theological Dictionary of the New Testament*, trans. G. W. Bromiley, 9 vols. (Grand Rapids: Eerdmans, 1964-1974).
7. Cf. for instance B. Oliver, "Depth Grammar as a Methodological Concept in Philosophy," *International Philosophical Quarterly* 12 (1972), 111-30; "The Ontological Structure of Linguistic Theory," *Monist* 53 (1969), 262-74; Philip Pettit, "Wittgenstein and the Case for Structuralism," *Journal of the British Society for Phenomenology* 3 (1972), 46-57; and Gary Phillips, "Wittgenstein and Chomsky: Some Implications of Linguistic Philosophy for a Structural Methodology," an unpublished paper prepared for the "Semiology and Exegesis Project," an interdisciplinary project at Vanderbilt University sponsored by the National Endowment for the Humanities.
8. The model for the narrative structure which we succinctly describe here has been established by A. J. Greimas and his followers. For a more detailed presentation of this model see, besides A. J. Greimas' work, J. Calloud, *L'Analyse structurale du récit* (Lyons: Profac, 1973); my forthcoming translation of this book, *Structural Analysis of Narrative;* and D. Patte, "An Analysis of Narrative Structure and the Good Samaritan," *Semeia* 2 (1974), 1-26.
9. These comments could be made about each of the structures discussed in this paper.
10. The actantial position "subject" should not be confused with the grammatical subject of a sentence.

11. It is to be noted that the initial sequence is not necessarily manifested at the beginning of a narrative text: the order in the text is determined by the style of the author and by the literary genre.
12. According to this understanding of the narrative structure what V. Propp termed the "main test" is the topical sequence and what he termed "qualifying test" and "glorifying test" are subsequences. Cf. V. Propp, *Morphology of the Folktale* (Austin: University of Texas, 1968).
13. For a more detailed analysis of the parable of the Good Samaritan in terms of the narrative structure see Daniel Patte, "An Analysis of Narrative Structure and the Good Samaritan," *Semeia* 2 (1974), 14-26. Cf. the rest of this issue (or other interpretations and discussions).
14. See the analysis of a part of a theological text—the epistle to the Galatians—in chapter 4 of my forthcoming book, *What is Structural Exegesis?* (Philadelphia: Fortress Press, in press).
15. Cf. C. Lévi-Strauss, *Mythologiques I. Le cru et le cuit* (Paris: Plon, 1964), Eng. trans., *The Raw and the Cooked* (New York: Harper and Row, 1969); *Mythologiques II. Du miel au cendre* (Paris: Plon, 1967); *Mythologiques III. L'origine des manières de table* (Paris: Plon, 1968); *Mythologiques IV. L'homme nu* (Paris: Plon, 1971).
16. Cf. C. Lévi-Strauss, "The Structural Study of Myth," *Structural Anthropology* (Garden City, N.Y.: Doubleday & Company, 1963).
17. Cf. Lévi-Strauss, *Structural Anthropology*, pp. 215-25. For simplicity's sake we only refer to one version of this myth (Stevenson's version). Lévi-Strauss was concerned to compare various versions.
18. Cf. Lévi-Strauss, *Structural Anthropology,* p. 221.
19. The following interpretation of the Zuñi myth is our own. Lévi-Strauss did not provide it.
20. The following remarks are intended as an illustration rather than a rigorous analysis. The very complexity of the Zuñi myth in its various versions would demand an extensive treatment which cannot be presented in the limits of this essay. It should be noted that Lévi-Strauss proposes this formula in order to express the relation between two formulations (two stories) of the same myth (e.g., the Zuñi myth). Our interpretation of Lévi-Strauss' formula is justified by the fact that, as discussed below, each story manifests only *one* pair of oppositions.
21. This is why a series of narrative-mythological texts is needed in order to invest significantly the mythical structure and the analyst needs to consider all the variants of each myth. Cf. Lévi-Strauss, *Structural Anthropology*, pp. 213-15.
22. Cf. Louis Marin, *Sémiotique de la Passion* (Bibliothèque des Sciences Religieuses; Paris: Aubier Montaigne and Cerf, 1971), Chapter 1.
23. For a discussion of the difference between contraries and contradictories see A. J. Greimas and F. Rastier, "The Interaction of Semiotic Constraints," *Yale French Studies* 41 (1969), 86-105.
24. Among the recent studies which interpret the parable of the Good Samaritan as an example story see Dan O. Via Jr., *The Parables* (Philadelphia: Fortress Press, 1967), p. 12; R. Bultmann, *The History of the Synoptic Tradition* (New York: Harper & Row, 1963), pp. 77-78.

JOURNEY INTO OBLIVION:
A Structural Analysis of Gen. 22:1-19

JAMES CRENSHAW

IN DUE TIME God put Abraham to the test. "Abraham," he said. "Yes," Abraham answered. God said to him, "Take, I beg of you, your only son, Isaac, whom you love, and go to the land of the Amorites.* There you shall sacrifice him upon one of the mountains that I declare to you." Now Abraham arose early in the morning, saddled his ass, and took along his two lads and Isaac his son. Having split wood for the sacrifice, he arose and went to the place God showed him. On the third day Abraham looked up and saw the place from a distance. He then instructed the lads: "Stay here with the ass. I and the lad† will go yonder; we shall worship, and we shall return to you." Now Abraham took the wood for the offering and put it upon his son Isaac. In his own hand he took the fire (stone) and the knife, and the two of them walked together.

Isaac said to his father Abraham, "Dad?" Abraham said, "Yes, son." Isaac said, "Lo, here are fire and wood, but where is the sacrificial lamb?" Abraham answered, "God will see to a lamb for the sacrifice, my son." And the two of them walked together.

*The Syriac reading is preferable to the Masoretic text's Moriah.
†Both the order and language are significant, although less felicetous than "the lad and I."

James L. Crenshaw, Professor of Old Testament at Vanderbilt Divinity School, is the author of *Prophetic Conflict* and editor of *Essays in Old Testament Ethics* and *Studies in Ancient Israelite Wisdom.* Along with Daniel Patte (who has an essay in this issue) he is recipient of an N.E.H. grant to institute an inter-disciplinary program in structuralism.

When they came to the place of which God told him, Abraham built there an altar, laid out the wood, bound Isaac his son, and placed him upon the altar on top of the wood. Then Abraham stretched out his hand and took the knife in order to slay his son. An angel of the Lord called to him from heaven, "Abraham, Abraham." "Yes?" Abraham answered. He said, "Do not stretch forth your hand against the lad, nor do anything to him, for now I know you are a god-fearing man, since you did not withhold from me your only son." Then Abraham looked and spied a* ram caught in the thicket by its horns. Abraham went, took the ram, and sacrificed it in place of his son. Then Abraham called the name of that place "The Lord provides," for it is said, "Today on the mountain the Lord was seen."

The angel of the Lord called to Abraham a second time from heaven, "I have sworn by myself, it is a whisper of the Lord, that because you have done this thing and have not withheld your only son, I shall surely bless you and multiply your progeny like the stars of heaven and the sand on the seashore. Your descendants will inherit the gates of their enemies, and all nations of the earth will bless themselves by your descendants, because you have obeyed my voice." Then Abraham returned to his lads, and they arose and went to Beersheba together. There Abraham remained.

A Son Sacrifices His Father (Gen. 12)

Monstrous! That word alone suffices in characterizing the divine imperative whispered in the ear of one who had earlier turned his back upon his father in answer to another startling command issued by God. Severed from every link with the past by his obedience to the imperative, "Go from your country and your kindred and your father's house to the land that I will show you," Abraham now hears the summons to give up all hope of a future. "Take, I beg of you, your son . . . There you shall sacrifice him upon one of the mountains that I declare to you." Bereft of both past and future, Abraham possesses the present alone, and it assumes the guise of a dreadful test. Past and future merge in a single word, the only apposition in the entire story. That word is *Isaac, whom you love*. Either way Abraham loses, whether he sacrifices his son or abandons his God. Small wonder

*Reading "one" instead of "behind," hence a ram.

he "moves about his grim task with silent resignation, as if he were an automaton."[1]

The break with past memories entails a long journey from abundance into scarcity and strains Abraham's patience to the breaking point. Time after time he takes matters into his own hands and places in jeopardy the threefold promise of land, progeny, and blessing. Driven from the promised land by hunger, he sacrifices his wife's honor, a subterfuge he finds useful more than once. Unable to abide by the divine timetable, Abraham hastens the birth of a son, Ishmael, and acquiesces when a jealous Sarah drives mother and son into the wilderness, thereby preparing her husband for yet another separation of father and son. Through all these wanderings from plenty into poverty, peace into strife, honor into shame, God upholds his chosen one and turns defeat into victory. Barrenness gives way to birth pangs, sorrow to rejoicing. She who abandoned all hope of conceiving at last laughs as tiny arms encircle her neck. Abraham, who left behind an aged father, now receives this child as token of God's faithfulness—but not for long, for God brooks no rivals.

A Father Sacrifices His Beloved Son (Gen. 22)

The very words with which God crushes a new-born paternal pride take Abraham on a journey into memories of that first severance of father and son. In each instance, Genesis 12 and 22, the imperative "Go" is followed by an unspecified place that God promises to make known to him in due time. In each account, too, the heart of the command pulses with a single word, *father* in one, *son* in the other. The narrative framework of Genesis 22 reinforces the association between the two imperatives. Januslike it looks back upon Genesis 12, both by its initial words and by the repetition of the original threefold promise at the end. The reminder of a past test leads to yet another one, this time identified by the narrator as such. Not privy to this precious bit of information that God intends no harm to Isaac,[2] Abraham, who had robbed his father of a son, is now called upon to take one final step. God asks nothing less from him than a trudging into the darkness of divine abandonment.[3] Isaac, also, walks beside his father toward some undeclared destiny, little suspecting that he starts out on a journey into oblivion. Overwhelming suspense fills the whole narrative, justifying the term epic.

The Journey into the Depths

On the surface, the journey is not a difficult one. Requiring but three days, perhaps more, the walk was hardly worth mentioning alongside routine trips in the ancient world, which often lasted for weeks or even months. This, however, is no ordinary journey from Beersheba to the unnamed mountain and back again to Beersheba. On the contrary, "the nightmare physical trial entrains . . . a boundless spiritual ordeal."[4] The language itself calls attention to the ordeal through which Abraham, and eventually Isaac, pass. With conscious avoidance of the destined site's name, save the initial Moriah which is textually uncertain,[5] the narrator uses surrogates like "there," "yonder," "the place that I will declare to you," and "that place."

Not everyone completes the journey to the chosen mountain. Sarah remains at Beersheba, blissfully ignorant of her husband's dreadful mission. The two lads accompanying Abraham and Isaac stop short of the mountain, and when they return to Beersheba they have not confronted anything but the ass. Abraham climbs the mountain, meets an angel of mercy, and returns to the lads, then to Sarah at Beersheba. Isaac also ascends the mountain, encounters a father intent upon murder,[6] walks into oblivion. Not a word is heard about his return; the text leaves him there. The situation can be described in the following way:

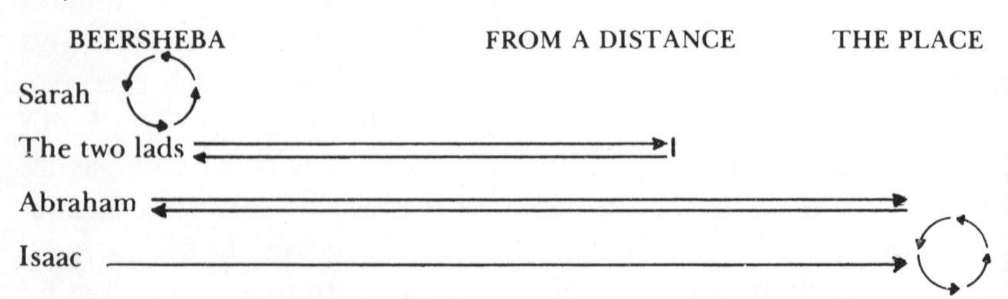

The rich vocabulary for the journey's destination finds its corollary in the climatic use of the verb *bo'* to designate the actual arrival at the site chosen by God, whereas the verb *halak* is used relentlessly everywhere else, even when one would expect another word, *ruṣ*. Surely Abraham *ran* to the ram and offered it in place of his son before God could change his mind again! Or should we think of a victory of the Satanic impulse within Abraham's breast? The thought that "if on high the mere *as though* is so highly regarded, imagine the power of *the actual*!"

must have tempered his enthusiasm.[7] After all, the ancient law demanding human sacrifice was never tampered with in the Covenant Code. It stands today in all its starkness: "The first-born you shall offer to me . . . " (Exod. 22:28, M.T.). Beside this statute from hoary antiquity lingers another, at least in common sentiment: "Without the shedding of blood there is no atonement."

The sole temporal reference in the narrative actually signifies ethical behavior: So exemplary is his conduct, Abraham rises early in the morning to obey the divine command. Likewise the allusion to the third day calls forth the mythical expectation of extraordinary happenings rather than the mere lapse of three days since leaving home.[8] At home in mythical expectation, too, is the rescue of Isaac *at the eleventh hour*, a prominent motif in Israelite legends.

The journey that leads from dawn to the dark night of the soul is commissioned by God (*'elohim*), who is mentioned five times. The nullification of the original command comes from *Yahweh*, who receives equal billing. No tension within God lurks beneath the surface, despite different names for God.[9] Significantly, *'elohim* speaks to Abraham as if on earth, but the angel of Yahweh must call out from heaven. The latter finds it necessary to name Abraham twice because of the distance separating them, the resolve with which the father seeks to carry out the divine command, or the heavy burden that dulls his senses as he readies the knife to draw precious blood. Two times God speaks to Abraham, and twice the angel of the Lord cries out to the obedient father.

The Sacrifice of the Will

Silence marks the journey from the first sighting of the mountain to its top, with a single exception. A refrain sets off the dialogue between father and son: "and the two of them walked together." Use of this refrain a third time in the final verse of the story suggests that the conversation between father and son provides the narrative's real center.[10] Perplexed by the presence of fire and wood, Isaac asks about the missing victim; yet in light of his father's designation of him as a lad, Isaac cannot bring himself to mention the knife. His poignant question forces Abraham to restore the normal form of address, "my son." Still it is conceivable that Abraham deceives his son in the enigmatic response, for the final "my son" may be used appositionally rather than as direct address. If such a reading is allowed, Abraham's response would be an instance of double entendre.[11] Isaac understands the words as a recognition of sonship, whereas Abraham secretly thinks of a sacrifice, namely his son.

The identification of Isaac with the lads forces the reader to ask still another question. Who are Abraham's two lads, and what is their role in the story? The use of *the lad* with Isaac as referent occurs in the father's words to the two lads who stop short of the ultimate destination, and in the initial words of the angel of the Lord. At least two possibilities present themselves. The two lads may be Ishmael and Eliezer, Abraham's two sons whom God has somehow forgotten. This would not be the first time Abraham only partially fulfilled the divine command, for he allowed his nephew to accompany the wandering family at an earlier time. Thus understood, the lads are reminders that other sons call Abraham father. God refuses, however, to take the bait and permit a substitution of one of them for Isaac. The second alternative is preferable: Abraham's reference to Isaac as the lad announces that he has already given up his beloved son in his heart. Small wonder Isaac utters those pregnant words: "Where is the lamb for the sacrifice?" for he perceives the significance of *hanna'ar*, the lad.

Syntagmatic Structure

Structural parallelism exists, too, in the use of accusatives. The imperative's malice stuns Abraham, embodying a threefold direct object in the same way that the ancient promise was three-dimensional. "Take . . . your son, your only one whom you love, Isaac . . ." Three signs of the accusative set off the objects of three different verbs in the awful description of Abraham's preparations for the final demonstration of obedience.[12] The somnambulistic nature of Abraham's actions arises from the agony stirring his soul; dazed, he erects there the altar, arranges the wood, binds his son Isaac.[13] Likewise, the account of the dreadful moment employs three signs of the accusative: he stretches out his hand and seizes the knife, in order to slay his son. A noteworthy shift from finite verb to infinitive takes place in the description of Abraham's intention. Thus one cannot miss the purpose of these actions described with such minute detail and in technical language of the sacrificial cult.

Twice Abraham lifts up his eyes from the ground; each time he spies something that evokes tumultuous feelings. This uplifted eye is the only gesture in three days. Suppressed is every sign of life excepting footfalls.[14] The first time he looks up, the mountain destined to receive his son looms large before him; the next time his eyes dare to look toward heaven Abraham sees the substitute sacrifice provided by God himself. Strangely no lifted eye searches for or acknowledges the presence of the source of the initial imperative or its extraordinary cancellation. Divine presence is almost taken for granted.

The Qualifying Test

In a sense the story bears the character of a qualifying test. The fulfillment of the promise articulated in Genesis 12 and reaffirmed at crucial stages during Abraham's journey through alien territory actualizes the divine intention to bless all nations by means of one man. Abraham's excessive love for the son of promise comes dangerously close to idolatry and frustrates the larger mission. Thus is set the stage for the qualifying test. The formal structure can be depicted in the following manner:

A. Semantic Narrative Sequence[15]

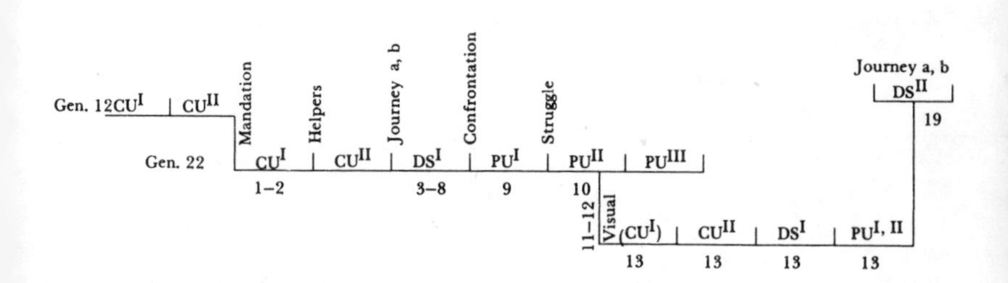

B. Canonical Functions

1–2 Mandation (contractual syntagm)
3–8 Departure (dusjunctional syntagm)
9–10 Arrival (performancial syntagm)
11–12 Mandation (contractual syntagm)
13 Communication (performancial syntagm II)
14 Attribution (qualification)
15–18 Communication (attribution)
19 Departure/Arrival (disjunctional syntagm)

Only once does the narrator surface, unless the initial sentence is so understood. Reflexive discourse characterizes the statement explaining the name of the memorable site. "Then Abraham called the name of that place 'The Lord provides,' for it is said, 'Today on the mountain the Lord was seen.' " One minor sequence also appears, namely Abraham's imperative addressed to the lads: "Stay here with the ass. I and the lad will go yonder; we shall worship, and we shall return to you." Helpers abound in the sequence: the two lads, the ass, fire, wood, knife, Isaac, the altar, a thicket, horns, and (the rope). Having successfully stood the test, Abraham hears the blessing affirmed anew. His victory over an inordinate love for Isaac equips Abraham once again to become an instrument of blessing to the nations. In the language of myth, the qualifying test has resulted in a restoration of the original situation. The movement is truly a *regressus ad initium.* The purpose of the test from God's perspective is epistemological, from Abraham's volitional. The successful completion of the test communicates knowledge to God, specifically, Abraham's willingness to give up his beloved son; indeed, he has already done so.

A mediation of opposites takes place on a number of levels. Foremost are:

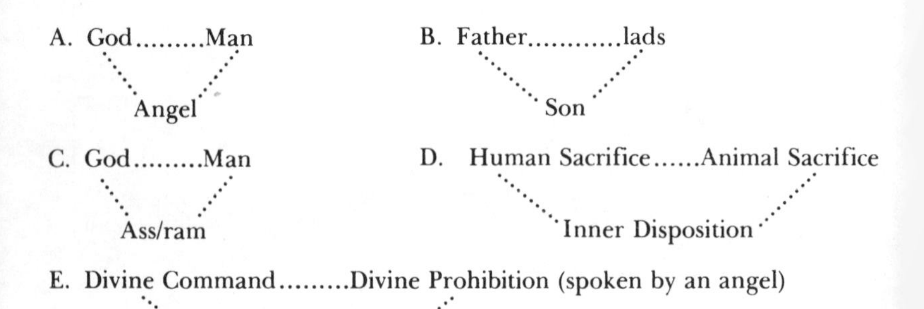

SYNTACTIC FEATURES

Affective terminology is used sparingly in the story. Once Isaac is described as the son whom Abraham loves, and this sentiment is strengthened by the thrice-repeated reference to him as an only son. The direct address in Abraham's answer to Isaac's hammer-like question also expresses endearment: "God will see to a lamb for the sacrifice, my son." Language of animosity or adversity is equally scarce. The divine command is actually called a test, and the renewed promise speaks of subjugation of enemies. The knife poised for the purpose of slaying Isaac is the supreme act of worship, and Abraham's surrender of his excessive love for his son demonstrates that he is a god-fearing man. Presumably such religion moves in the affective dimension of life.

Puns penetrate the narrative from beginning to end. Since the father becomes an enemy to his son, the unexpected allusion to enemies (*'oyebaw*) in the repetition of the promise recalls the frequent references to a father (*'ab, 'abi, 'abiw*). Other similarities are probably intentional too: *hanna 'ar* [the lad] and *sha 'ar* [gate]; *sham* [there], *shem* [name], *hashshamayim* [the heavens]; *b*^{e}*ni* [my son], *b*^{e}*no* [his son], *bin*^{e}*ka* [your son], *wayyiben* [and he built]; *sh*^{e}*bu* [stay], *w*^{e}*nashubah* [and we shall return], *yesheb* [he dwelt]; and *'aḥar* [behind], *ne'*^{e}*ḥaz* [caught]. The name that Abraham gives to the holy place enshrouds at least four puns (*yir'eh* [he will see], *yera'eh* [he was seen], *y*^{e}*re'* [one who fears], *wayyar'* [and he saw]).

The story is rich in anticipation. The mountain is called the place that God will make known, or simply "there." The lamb caught in a thicket is foreshadowed long before, and Abraham's return to his lads is specifically promised. In each instance the actual realization brings a surprise. The place of the dreadful act becomes a scene of divine mercy, the lamb is providentially supplied by a satisfied deity, and the lone appearance of Abraham eclipses any anticipation that both father and son will return.[16] The birth of so many surprises prepares the way for the last one, God's cancellation of the original mandate.

The story makes use of an economy of words. Amidst such "background," redundancy rarely appears.[17] Exceptions are the following: *and he said* (vv. 2,7), *and lo* (v. 13), *whisper of the Lord* (v. 16), *and Abraham* (v. 7), or *his father* (v. 7). Restraint characterizes the narrative. Here one encounters fragmentary speeches, silence, reticence. God always recedes into the depths, without explaining the reason for the test. Abraham's earlier boldness in arguing with God (Gen. 18) produces no protest here, not even a clenched fist or bitten lip. Isaac conceals his awful suspicion; no word is spoken of the effect on his life. Has he lost faith in God and in his father? No explanation for the angel's cancellation of the divine decree is given, and no mention of Sarah's response to the good news that her son is alive and well.[18] Most astonishingly, we do not hear a word of rejoicing when the ordeal is ended by an urgent command: "Do not stretch forth your hand against the lad, nor do anything to him."

Formulaic expressions enrich the vocabulary of the narrative. "The short and simple sentence, 'And the two of them walked on together' (8) covers what is perhaps the most poignant and eloquent silence in all literature."[19] During this brief journey of father and son, the father demonstrates his affection by carrying the dangerous items, namely the fire and the knife.[20] Isaac bears the heavy load of wood upon his shoulders, unaware that soon he will be stretched out across the sticks. Yet now he must know his father's true intentions. "The pathos of this dialogue is inimitable: the artless curiosity of the child, the irrepressible affection of the father, and the stern ambiguity of his reply, can hardly be read without tears."[21] Another formula emphasizes the complete dependence of Abraham upon God, even for the identification of the place "that God will show him." Once this expression adorns God's lips, twice the narrator's.

At least one formulaic expression from the broader canonical literature appears in this brief story. "Now I know that you are a man who fears God" is a variant of a formula of discovery often used in prophetic literature, particularly in the Book of Ezekiel. The threefold promise, also, is couched in formulaic language, rich in metaphoric substance. A related stylistic device, repetition, finds expression too. Noteworthy is the repetition of "he stretched out his hand," "you have not withheld from me your only son," and "offer up your/his son."

The meaning of words does not remain constant in the story. A striking example of such a shift in sense is found in the everyday word, *wayyikra'* (and he called). The two occasions in which the angel cries out differ considerably from the narrator's reflective comment: "Then Abraham called the name of that place, 'The Lord sees,' for it is said, 'Today on the mountain the Lord is seen.' "[22] By what stretch of the imagination can one say God was seen on the mountain? Surely the narrator does not identify the ram and God, although Abraham would be justified in slaying the ram were such the case.

MYTHICAL STRUCTURE (Gen. 22 and Isa. 7)

On a deeper level the conflict depicted in Genesis 22 bears witness to opposing forces: father versus son, parental love versus fear of the gods, and intention versus actual deed. The trained ear can barely distinguish an echo of the Oedipal struggle: in it Abraham abandons his father in favor of a higher allegiance. Perhaps, too, the silence of the story about his encounter with a father bent on murder conceals a resultant animosity between father and son.[23] On the other hand, the narrator takes great pains to demonstrate Abraham's love for Isaac, thereby signifying the monstrosity of the test imposed upon one who has waited so long for the fulfillment of the divine promise.

From time immemorial religious man asked what the gods require of him. The obvious answer came to him early: that which is most precious. Such intuition manifests itself as fertility worship and human sacrifice. Even in Israel, where religious consciousness transcends both impulses, "age-old beliefs continued to nest in the thickets of the soul."[24] Consequently, troubled times witness renewed worship at the cults of sacral sex or child sacrifice. Dire straits bestow new life upon the idolatrous impulse: perhaps after all God demands human sacrifice, as the old law stipulates. When the son destined for fire embodies divine faithfulness, the pathos of the struggle between parental love and fear of the gods fills every syllable of the story. Significantly, Abraham's obedience convinces God once and for all that in him a proper fear resides.

Conflict of another sort underlies the text in its present form. A distinction between intention and actual deed enters the religious dimension. No rare insight, such a distinction appears in ancient Egyptian instructions, and pervades Israel's prophetic oracles. Eventually the knowledge that God cares more for inner disposition than outer manifestation enriches the vocabulary of Israel's religious leaders, for whom circumcision of the heart becomes an apt metaphor. In Abraham's case, the willingness to sacrifice his beloved son suffices for the deed itself: "because you have done this thing and have not withheld your only son. . . ."

Inasmuch as the author chose his words with utmost care, the particle of entreaty in the initial imperative merits close examination. Only twice in the entire corpus of biblical literature does *na'* appear in a divine command.[25] Its rarity compels us to examine the text for something that may otherwise be hidden from view. What function does the particle of entreaty serve? Does it not underline the monstrosity of the command, communicating to the attentive listener that God knows the nature of the request whispered in Abraham's ear? If so, a translation ought to take note of an element of imploring within the divine command: "Take your son, *I beg of you*, and offer him up. . . ."[26] The other use of *na'* in a divine imperative also occurs in the context of an endangered son. Here God commands Isaiah to take his son, who is himself a walking promise of weal or woe, and to pose a test of trust to none other than King Ahaz. This monarch, one of two kings in Israel who reportedly offered their sons by fire, had already shown the poverty of his faith by sending to Assyria for military assistance rather than place his trust in the Lord. In this account of Isaiah and his son, the word *nisah* leaps to view, this time on pious lips. When prodded to put God to the test, Ahaz interjects: "I will not ask, and I will not *tempt* the Lord." Angrily the prophet pronounces a sign: "Behold, the young woman is pregnant and will bear a son, and will call his name 'With-us-is-God.' " This stinging message found its way into the Christian proclamation of still another sacrifice of a beloved son at the hands of his Father. He who once knew the ecstasy of obedience on another's part now experiences the agony of ultimate sacrifice.[27]

NOTES

1. George Coats, "Abraham's Sacrifice of Faith. A Form-Critical Study of Genesis 22," *Interpretation*, 27 (1973), 397.
2. Henning Graf Reventlow, *Opfere deinen Sohn, Biblische Studien*, 53 (Neukirchen-Vluyn: Neukirchener Verlag des Erziehungsvereins, 1968), 69 perceives the tragic irony of the narrative, for the reader knows God is *merely* testing the hero, for whom suspense mounts to the last moment.
3. Gerhard von Rad, *Das Opfer des Abraham* (München: C. Kaiser Verlag, 1971), pp. 32, 40, and *Genesis* (London: SCM Press, 1961), p. 239.
4. E. A. Speiser, *Genesis* (Anchor Bible; Garden City, N.Y.: Doubleday & Company, Inc., 1964), p. 164.
5. Several versions reflect a form of the verb "to see," anticipating Abraham's ambiguous response to Isaac's searing question ("The Lord will see to a sacrificial lamb, my son") and the narrator's reflective comment ("Then Abraham called the name of that place 'The Lord provides,' for it is said, 'Today on the mountain the Lord was seen' ").

6. The transformation of Abraham's visage is brought out in unforgettable pathos by Søren Kierkegaard in *Fear and Trembling* (Garden City, N.Y.: Doubleday & Company, Inc., 1941), p. 27. Rembrandt succeeds in putting this complexity of human emotions onto canvas. For Rembrandt's interpretation of the events in Gen. 22, see von Rad, *Das Opfer des Abraham*, pp. 86-94.
7. Shalom Spiegel, *The Last Trial* (New York: Schocken Books, 1967), p. 78.
8. George M. Landes, "The 'Three Days and Three Nights' Motif in Jonah 2:1," *Journal of Biblical Literature*, 86 (1967), 446-50.
9. Rabbinic literature distinguishes between the names *'elohim* and *YHWH* in terms of qualities of justice and mercy respectively. For discussion of another solution (different sources, oral or written), see, besides the relevant commentaries, Reventlow, *Opfere deinen Sohn,* and Rudolf Kilian, *Isaaks Opferung, Stuttgarter Bibel-Studien* 44 (Stuttgart: Verlag Katholisches Bibelwerk, 1970). The reigning theory of an Elohistic narrative (1-14, 19) and a Yahwistic supplement (15-18) by one who did not consider the sparing of Isaac ample reward for Abraham's supreme act of obedience remains problematical. Kilian, *Isaaks Opferung*, pp. 124-25 envisions five stages through which the story passed. According to him, a cultic aetiology becomes a story about deliverance of a beloved son, which in turn is adapted to the patriarchal traditions, turned by the Elohist into a test with paradigmatic import, and localized at the site of the Jerusalem temple.
10. Reventlow, *Opfere deinen Sohn,* pp. 43-44, perceives the significance of dialogue in the story. He writes of two stages of dialogue between God and Abraham, with human discourse as the center of the story. Reventlow thinks of the relationship between father and son and the affinity for twos and threes as noteworthy features of this epic narrative (cf. Kilian, *Isaaks Opferung*, pp. 90-99).
11. In short, the ambiguity of Abraham's answer, "God will see to (provide) a lamb," continues in the words, "my son." Such deception is also found in verse 5, where Abraham tells the lads that the purpose of the trip is to worship, and promises that both he and Isaac will return.
12. To be sure, a fourth sign of the accusative occurs, but it has a pronominal object.
13. Von Rad, *Genesis*, p. 236, calls attention to the staccato-like sentences describing Abraham's preparations for the sacrifice.
14. Erich Auerbach, *Mimesis* (Princeton: Princeton University Press, 1953), p. 10.
15. The terminology is borrowed from Vladimir Propp, *Morphology of the Folktale* (Austin, Texas and London: University of Texas Press, 1968) and the revision of Propp's categories by A. J. Greimas, *Du sens: Essais sémiotiques* (Paris: Seuil, 1970). See also Jean Calloud, *L'analyse structurale du récit* (Lyon: Publications de la faculté de théologie, 1973).
16. Spiegel, *The Last Trial*, pp. 3-4, discusses rabbinic speculation about Isaac's failure to return with his father. Even if the original story did not conclude with the actual sacrifice of Isaac, such a view arose early in the Jewish community, flourishing during perilous times.
17. Thatic discourse is no argument against the economical use of words, for it is built into the very structure of the Hebrew language, particularly cases of hendiadys (vv. 3, 19 "arose and went"). Auerbach perceives the economical character of the narrative, a tendency to leave to the imagination everything but bare essentials. He describes the story as "fraught with background" (*Mimesis*, p. 12).

18. After hearing the report of Abraham's ordeal, according to rabbinic legend, Sarah cries out six times and expires (Strack-Billerbeck, *Kommentar zum Neuen Testament aus Talmud und Midrasch*, Bd. IV, pp. 181-82).
19. Speiser, *Genesis*, p. 165.
20. Hermann Gunkel, *Genesis* (Göttingen: Vandenhoeck & Ruprecht, 1901), p. 237.
21. John Skinner, *Genesis* (International Critical Commentary; Edinburgh: T. & T. Clark, 1901), pp. 329-30.
22. *Yahweh yire'* is anticipated in verse 8 (*'elohim yire'*), although the Masoretic pointing recalls Moriah of verse 2 (*yera'e*).
23. On the conflict between father and son, see the essay by Leszek Kolakowski, "Abraham oder eine höhere Trauer," printed by von Rad in *Das Opfer des Abraham*, pp. 81-85.
24. Spiegel, *The Last Trial*, p. 77.
25. Brown, Driver & Briggs, *A Hebrew and English Lexicon of the Old Testament* (Oxford: Clarendon Press, 1907), p. 609.
26. Rashi takes note of the petitionary language in this verse and offers a theological explanation for it (Sanhedrin 89b). I am indebted to Rabbi Aaron Michelson for this reminder that there is nothing new under the sun.
27. Like the noble mother of seven martyrs (II Macc. 7), God can say to Abraham: "Yours were the trials; mine were the performances." On this theme see Spiegel, *The Last Trial*, pp. 13-16 and *passim*.

CRITICISM AND METHOD:
Hirsch, Frye, Barthes

EVAN WATKINS

I

LITERARY CRITICISM for the last twenty years has been preoccupied with the possibility of method in a way which is strikingly new. A traditional conception of methodology intends its use as provisional and heuristic, to organize the content of experience into meaningful patterns, but in a way that could always be qualified by further evidence. Contemporary critical methods more often than not posit as a goal the organization of other methods. The promise is that method can become a self-regulatory and self-contained system. The question presupposed within that promise must be developed explicitly, however. It is not enough to "illuminate" the "field" of literature by "synoptic thought." Literature is not a field, method is not a spotlight, and criticism is not a mode of vision. To think so is to reduce the felt intricacy of human activities to a mere model which is embarrassingly vague at best. A method cannot be so easily severed from an aesthetics and a philosophy.

The common feature in the new methodologies of criticism is the attempt of each to found itself on a distinction conceived as fundamental. At the very beginning of *Validity in Interpretation,* E. D. Hirsch distinguishes meaning from significance, and the subsequent elaboration of the argument depends absolutely on the intransigence with which that division is initiated. It is what

Mr. Watkins is an Assistant Professor of English at Michigan State University, having completed the Ph.D. at the University of Iowa in 1972. He teaches courses in critical theory, including structuralism, and is presently working on a book on contemporary critical theory.

makes possible a logic of validation designed to adjudicate objectively among various constructions of textual meaning. Such logic is not mere method; its task is to decide which "guess" or pseudo-method has produced the most probably correct results. Northrop Frye at the beginning of *Anatomy of Criticism* insists that criticism must choose as a goal the knowledge of literature as something wholly distinct from value judgments about individual works, and only knowledge based on a conception of a total form of literature can be certain. So his contempt for "taking a stand": "One's definite position is one's weakness, the source of one's liability to error and prejudice, and to gain adherents to a definite position is only to multiply one's weakness like an infection" (*AC*, 19).[1] *Anatomy* is to be construed not as merely one more method, but as the means whereby all particular methods may be integrated. Roland Barthes, likewise, has nothing but contempt for the "academic" historical method, as being the product of a vested interest in a particular social structure. Linguistics, on the other hand, offers the possibility for a "general form" of discourse and a "criticism of criticisms" (*CE*, 275) based on the distinction between the "system" of a text and its "message."

But the attempt to begin with a distinction has always involved a paradox. The classic way to pose the problem asks by what means the "fundamental" distinction is effected and who institutes the means. This predisposes the answer toward a philosophy of reflection and toward a formulation such as Kant's antinomy:

> *Thesis*: The judgment of taste is not based upon concepts; for otherwise it would admit of dispute (would be determinable by proofs).
>
> *Antithesis*: The judgment of taste is based upon concepts; for otherwise, in spite of its diversity, we could not quarrel about it (we could not claim for our judgment the necessary assent of others).

The resolution reveals the means by which the judgment of taste can be distinguished from other forms of thought, and ultimately the procedure comes to rest—and here Husserl joins Kant—in the unity of the subject as the substantial origin of all distinction.

Italian criticism in the early part of the twentieth century developed the first coherent aesthetics to challenge the assumptions implicit in reflective thought, noting that the way in which the question is asked itself presupposes a difference which then cannot be accounted for. It is impossible for a reflective philosophy to explain its most elemental relation, that between the self-identity of a necessary subject, a thinking substance, and the multiplicity and contingency of what is thought about. To begin with a radical distinction is to imply the impossibility of ever reintegrating the terms of the disjunction. The alternative is an attempt to understand the relation between unity and multiplicity, necessity and contingency, as prior to any distinction which would privilege one term in itself. Croce, for example, insisted that any thinking through of a methodological distinction must involve its own activity in the resolution. Giovanni Gentile took the next step, arguing for an actual rather than a substantial origin, for a dialectically unifying act of thinking which develops in its critical alterity to itself. For Gentile the only necessity is in this act of thinking, not in an imaginary thinking substance or an imaginary object already there to be thought about. Thought is contingency in the act of becoming necessary by recognizing its own limitations. But because its origin is understood as actual rather than substantial, this movement can never be stilled; thought can never attain the security of taking full possession of its impassioned inner development by a reflective process of objectification. Necessity inheres in the very insecurity of the act of becoming rather than always being deferred in the illusory fullness and security of a *telos* lying just beyond the horizon of thought.[2]

While Croce's aesthetics, at least, has been valuable to the theoretical elaboration of the New Criticism by Eliseo Vivas and Murray Krieger, the forms of contemporary criticism with which I am concerned have developed a quite different criticism and a quite different resolution. The criticism is directed at the arbitrariness of a substantial subject as the source of distinction. There is no reason a process of reflection should end in a subject. Why not a further subject which reflects on the first subject, so that we may truly have knowledge of it, and then still a further subject which reflects on the first two so that we may have knowledge of them, a *partes extra partes* series *ad infinitum*? The resolution is to stay within the confines of reflective thought by beginning with a radical separation between what is necessary and what is contingent, but to do so by substituting a conception of a virtual for a substantial origin. I am going to argue that this resolution is the operative force in the work of Hirsch, Frye, and Barthes, and that it is the means by which they hope to institute a methodological formalism that can be self-regulatory.

I take my definition of "virtual" from another discipline, but one in which its meaning has been most explicitly recognized, in Lévi-Strauss' *The Raw and the Cooked*:

> But unlike philosophical reflection, which claims to go back to its own source ["directly" is understood in the French text], the reflections we are dealing with here concern rays whose only source is hypothetical ["*virtuel*" is the French word at this point, and I have preserved a literal translation]. Divergence of sequences and themes is a fundamental characteristic of mythological thought, which manifests itself as an irradiation; by measuring the directions and angles of the rays, we are led to postulate their common origin, as an ideal point on which those deflected by the structure of the myth would have converged had they not started, precisely, from some other point and remained parallel throughout their entire course (*RC*, 5-6; my brackets).

This "ideal point" leads to a structure elaborated by the observer, intended to approximate as closely as possible the movement of the mythic material, but at a necessary remove from it, a virtual distance. A little farther on, Lévi-Strauss explains why this is so and how he has responded to it:

> As the myths themselves are based on secondary codes (the primary codes being those that provide the substance of language [*ceux en quoi consiste le langage*]), the present work is put forward as a tentative draft of a tertiary code, which is intended to ensure the reciprocal translatability of several myths. This is why it would not be wrong to consider this book itself as a myth: it is, as it were, the myth of mythology (*RC,* 12; my brackets).

A claim for a "real," substantial origin would be an arbitrary imposition by the observer on the material of myth. On the other hand, a methodology which could trace the relationships among the forms of myth by assuming a mythic shape itself would be far more important, even though it could claim only a methodological and not a truth-value. Almost at the end of the book, the initial break with the conception of a substantial origin is emphatically affirmed:

> And if it is now asked to what final meaning these mutually significative meanings are referring—since in the last resort and in their totality they must refer to something—the only reply to emerge from this study is that myths signify the mind [*l'esprit*] that evolves

> them by making use of the world of which it is itself a part (*RC*, 341; my brackets).

Myth signifies the making of myth, and to halt the process at any one point, at the subject or at the world, claiming it as an origin, would be nothing more than an arbitrary imposition.

The initial advantage of developing a conception of a virtual origin for a methodology of literary criticism would seem to be that it can sanction a founding distinction and the impersonal objectivity of knowledge which can follow, while at the same time it avoids the need to explain the "real" relation between a necessary and self-identical subject and a contingent, multiple world. There is no longer any "real" subject, any author or any critic. Instead, there is the concept of "type" in Hirsch, of "archetype" in Frye, and of "metalanguage" in Barthes, a sequence I find to reveal with increasing clarity the presuppositions and limitations of the effort.

Despite the manifold differences, the central concern in both Hirsch and Frye is to develop a concept which can provide a determinate goal for literary criticism as a progressive and systematic discipline. This goal is conceived as the point at which no further change or transformation is permitted; it is stable and self-identical. Hirsch, for example, admits a potential infinity of interpretive constructions of meaning: "There are no methods for making guesses, no rules for generating insights" (*VI*, 203). But interpretation as a discipline represents the attempt to determine a means of eliminating error by taking as a subject these very interpretive constructions rather than the text itself, the relation of author to text, or the relation of text to reader. A method based on the text alone dissolves into the vagaries of "semantic autonomy," one based on the relation of author to text into the necessarily inconclusive attempts to determine with certainty the psychology of the author, and one based on the relation of text to reader into the relativism of mere taste. Hirsch's effort is to be limited to what happens after the "guesswork" of understanding: "the discipline of interpretation is founded, then, not on a methodology of construction but on a logic of validation" (*VI*, 207). Already constructed meanings, not the way in which those meanings came into existence, are what can be known. Meaning is thus what I have defined as "virtual," resulting from an ideal goal at an absolute remove from the problematic context of originating meaning, and from an attempt at understanding that origination of meaning or the significance, the value of the meaning.

Similarly, Frye has no explicit intention of decreeing one definitive method for the critic to employ: "The presence of incommunicable experience in the center of criticism will always keep criticism an art, as long as the critic recognizes that criticism comes out of it but cannot be built on it" (*AC*, 27-28). Knowledge of literature is "built on" a "central hypothesis" which can explain its own conceptual framework:

> Its materials, the masterpieces of literature, are not yet regarded as phenomena to be explained in terms of a conceptual framework *which criticism alone possesses*. They are still regarded as somehow constituting the framework or structure of criticism as well. I suggest that it is time for criticism to leap to a new ground from which it can discover what the organizing or containing forms of its conceptual framework are (*AC*, 15-16; italics mine).

This "new ground" for knowledge, like Hirsch's "meaning," is thus virtual, existing at a remove from the substance of its effort. Understanding literature is a potentially infinite task; what can be known is the virtual framework that renders such understanding intelligible and communicable.

The question both Hirsch and Frye must answer, then, is this: If meaning or knowledge is virtual—if it exists at a remove from the doubtful context of significance or value—are all discourses on a work equivalent? How can a methodology perform the task of judgment? I do not think the question can be posed this way by either of them, for it is precisely the concept of "judgment" that has been put out of play by the initial distinctions meaning/significance and knowledge/value-judgments. It has been replaced by a notion of "type" or "archetype" as an "identity," a point at which difference, and hence the necessity to choose, has been eliminated.

For Barthes, as for Lévi-Strauss in *The Raw and the Cooked*, the possibility of achieving such an identity is by its very nature problematical, implying nothing more than a return to the arbitrariness of a substantial subject as the undifferentiated source of distinction. For while the substitution of "virtual" for "substantial" may put at a distance any explanation of the relation between subject and world—between author and text or between reader and text—it must still face the problem of explaining the relation beween necessity and contingency, self-identity and multiplicity, and a conception of a necessary and stable identity becomes merely an hypostasis of the paradox and not a resolution. Thus Barthes must be content with a "presence," an identity that is always deferred, a metalanguage which fails in the very moment of its successful determination by introducing a movement of difference into the heart of its identity in a way that cannot be accounted for but only be repeated *ad infinitum*.

I do not wish my argument to imply that Italian criticism, the aesthetics of Croce and Gentile, can be reinaugurated as the last word for criticism. My implicit assumption, indeed, will be that their work represents a more convincing recovery from the postulates of reflective philosophy than the criticism which seems to me to dominate contemporary thought, but there are of course two propositions contained here: that in fact Italian aesthetics does offer a radical break from the problems of reflective thought, and that the criticism of Hirsch, Frye and Barthes does not. It is the second I shall be concerned to demonstrate. Nevertheless, the problems to be dealt with, I am convinced, are crucial; and if they are, Italian aesthetics can open the theoretical choices beyond the closure which results from the sequence of thought I shall be criticizing.

II

The immediate problem Hirsch faces in *Validity in Interpretation* is to define meaning in such a way as to preserve the clear implication of self-identity: "*Meaning* is that which is represented by the text; it is what the author meant by his use of a particular sign sequence; it is what the signs represent. *Significance*, on the other hand, names a relationship between that meaning and a person, or a conception, or a situation, or indeed anything imaginable" (*VI,* 8). Yet even here meaning, too, is a relation; it is that which must be *re*-presented in language, even if not necessarily the same language each time. Meaning occurs at the juncture of "a particular sign sequence" and an author's intention. The striking gesture which actually inaugurates the argument of *Validity in Interpretation* is Hirsch's attempt to neutralize this duality by installing meaning immediately within the concept of *type* as an "identity" which shares in both terms of an opposition, but never belongs wholly to either one: "It is essential to emphasize the concept of type since it is only through this concept that verbal meaning can be (as it is) a determinate object of consciousness and yet transcend (as it does) the actual contents of consciousness" (*VI*, 49). A type cannot be a purely linguistic construct, a sign, even though it signifies the content of the work. But neither can it be a kind of mental signifier, for it is itself "chosen" by an act of consciousness. It is to be conceived as "outside" this opposition, and indeed, as the identity which "governs" and "mediates" it: "Between the enormously broad system of types and possibilities that constitute a language, and the individual speech acts that have made it and continue to make it, there are mediating type concepts which govern particular utterances as meaningful wholes" (*VI*, 111).

As it pertains to verbal meaning, Hirsch's type thus stands in a critical relation to the three traditional conceptions of type: as ontological, constitutive, or heuristic; as a merely formal means of classification; and as historically determined. Hirsch diverges from the German tradition of hermeneutics in Heidegger and Gadamer because of this last requirement. To admit an historical constitution would be to allow all the forms of contingency which Hirsch wishes to exclude:

> The historicity of all interpretations is an undoubted fact, because the historical givens with which an interpreter must reckon—the language and the concerns of his audience—vary from age to age. However, this by no means implies that the meaning of a text varies from age to age, or that anybody who has done whatever is required to understand that meaning, understands a different meaning from his predecessors of an earlier age (*VI*, 137).

He must also diverge from neo-Kantian thought by denying that type is constitutive of, or a heuristic instrument pointing to, a substantial reality:

> On the other hand, the incongruity between the complete explicitness of things and the incomplete explicitness of our conceptions about them does not necessarily obtain when the thing we are concerned to know is a verbal meaning. Here full congruity [between type and meaning] is possible because meanings, being themselves types, are capable of being fully known (*VI*, 273).

Yet the refusal of these traditional sanctions for the concept of type in no way implies something that is merely arbitrary, a means of classification: " . . . for purposes of classification it matters very little whether we use Roman numerals, the weeks of the year, or the phases of the moon" (*VI*, 111), but type matters so much that it cannot be resolved even into a function of *langue*. Saussure's concept is based upon the assumption that the relation between signifier and signified in the sign is always purely arbitrary, and for Hirsch the relation between author's intention and sign sequence in a type cannot finally be arbitrary.

Having put aside these traditional senses of type, the question remains as to what means a logic of validation can employ to argue one type as more valid than another. The answer is a double one, given in a way that reveals the effaced duality of consciousness and language at the heart of the definition of type. Meaning is said on the one hand to be "an affair of consciousness" (*VI*, 37). The words are mere "physical tokens" apart from the consciousness of the author or the interpreter, and "only one interpretive problem can be answered with objectivity: 'What, in all probability, did the author mean to convey?' " (*VI,* 207) On the other hand, it is a type, in its particularity as a specific genre, "a sense of the whole," which constitutes every utterance:

> A genre conception is constitutive of speaking as well as of interpreting, and *it is by virtue of this that the genre concept sheds its arbitrary and variable character* . . . it is obvious that not only understanding but also speaking must be governed and constituted by a sense of the whole utterance (*VI*, 78; italics mine).

The author "wills" *this* particular meaning rather than that one, but that very spoken meaning is itself constituted by a sense of type, not by the author. Thus the validity of an interpreter's construction of meaning depends on his having acted *as if* the author were a substantial subject who inaugurated *this* meaning for his text and simultaneously *as if* the language of the text formed a linguistic system to be understood independently of the author, although neither, strictly speaking, is accurate. What can be accurate is a concept of type which somehow subsumes these two operations within itself as an "identity" existing independent of the interpreter's critical judgment. If it does not, then the authority for determining one construction of meaning as more valid than another is arbitrary.

Now, even granting that there is to be an absolute gap between "psychic processes" and intended meaning—in order to avoid a regression into the dubious territory of the psychology of the author—the logic of validation in any given case can never indicate exactly where that gap occurs because one of the two terms remains in principle unknowable. It is an impenetrable psyche, the subject of mere "guesswork." For Hirsch, the conventions of language are what can be known. But these conventions cannot originate this meaning, the authorial will-to-speak-meaning. Type, then, is in effect a no man's land between an unknowable psyche with its mysterious will-to-mean and mere "physical tokens," the already-spoken-meaning, arranged in helpful patterns by various interpretive monads which approach them. What everybody sees is said to be the "same," a typal identity of the author's will-to-mean and the linguistic already-spoken-meaning, but nobody can know for sure what it is he sees, this elusive "speaking" type which conjoins them. And he can hardly know what another sees.

It is not a question of a continuum, of one type being recognized as more probable than another. The absolute necessity, the non-arbitrariness of type as a general concept is immediately identical with the absolute contingency of any particular type, the arbitrariness of the interpreter who asserts that in *this* case the will-to-mean and the already-spoken-meaning represent *this* type. This immediate identity of necessity and contingency is the only self-identity possible in *Validity in Interpretation*. There is thus no way to judge the possible correctness of an interpretive conclusion; all constructions of meaning are equal.

The point of a more recent essay, "Three Dimensions of Hermeneutics," is that all discourses on the meaning of a text are in fact equivalent unless there is an agreement on an ethical norm between interpreters. If meaning is to be an analytical concept, then all meanings are equally real:

> One meaning of a text can have no higher claim than another on the grounds that it derives from the "nature of interpretation," for all interpreted meanings are ontologically equal; they are all equally real. When we discriminate between legitimate and illegitimate meanings in "Lycidas," for example, we cannot claim merely to be describing the nature of Milton's text, for the text compliantly changes its nature from one interpreter to another (*Three*, 246-47).

If a norm is agreed upon, then there is still the possibility for an objective reconstruction of meaning within the agreed-upon principle, and Hirsch attempts to make a case for authorial meaning as the one we *should* embrace. But for Hirsch to have given up so much is to lose any way of absolutely distinguishing meaning from significance, even though he does make an attempt:

> An interpreter is always playing two roles simultaneously—as speaker (or re-speaker) of meaning and as listener to meaning. Both moments are necessary, for if the text is not "spoken" (construed) it cannot be "heard," and if it is not heard, it cannot have been, for the interpreter, spoken. Meaning is what an interpreter actualizes from a text; significance is that actual speaking as heard in a chosen and variable context of the interpreter's experiential world (*Three*, 250).

This is a good statement with which to begin to understand the relation between meaning and significance as necessary and prior to their division, but it will not work to enforce an absolute distinction on which to base a theory of interpretation. After having engaged in the activity of both speaking and listening to myself speak, can I then reflect on my utterance and logically divide it into a moment of speaking—meaning—and a moment of listening—significance—which are utterly distinct? If so, then my act of reflection on the original utterance as I try to explain it would itself be both a speaking and a listening. Hence meaning never could be wholly free from the radically unstable context of significance in the way Hirsch desires, for each act that would divide meaning from significance would necessarily be compounded of both. And such an infinite series of contingent constructions is precisely the problem which the substitution of a virtual for a substantial origin of interpretation in *Validity in Interpretation* was to have eliminated.

I have said that Northrop Frye shares with Hirsch a central concern for criticism as a progressive and systematic discipline and that the concept of archetype, like type, projects an identity which is to efface the necessity for judgment by providing the possibility of a self-regulating system. Nevertheless, "archetype" is not merely a transposition of the problem Hirsch faces to a new level of inquiry. The etymological distinction between type and archetype suggests the possibility, but the underlying development of Frye's thinking results from a tension between two fundamentally different ways of conceiving the origination of criticism, a problem Hirsch feels he has displaced at the very beginning of his effort as all "guesswork" (hence he can say of Frye's thought that it belongs to "some theory about man" [*VI*, 110n], as if his own didn't).

Here is Frye at the end of "The Road of Excess":

> In Blake there is no either/or dialectic where one must be either a detached spectator or a preoccupied actor. Hence there is no divi-

> sion, though there may be a distinction, between the creative power of shaping the form and the critical power of seeing the world it belongs to. Any division instantly makes art barbaric and the knowledge of it pedantic—a bound Orc and a bewildered Urizen, to use Blake's symbols. The vision inspires the act, and the act realizes the vision. This is the most thorough-going view of the partnership of creation and criticism in literature I know, but for me, though other views may seem more reasonable and more plausible for a time, it is in the long run the only one that will hold (*SS*, 174).

What Frye characterizes as an "either/or dialectic" is of course not dialectical at all, but the seminal operation of classificatory thought. Classes can be made by definition mutually exclusive. This individual animal is either a sheep or a goat; this poetic image is either apocalyptic or demonic. The critic is either a disinterested spectator or a partisan polemicist. Implicit in the comment on Blake, on the other hand, is an incipient but genuine dialectic. Criticism of Blake, such as Frye's magnificent *Fearful Symmetry*, could hardly be content with placing a poem of his within an exclusive class of poems. Instead, it would have to show how all its rich individuality is a concrete realization of a universal form, and how Blake's creating the poem is at once a making and a knowing, creation and criticism. These opposites would be identified dialectically and not immediately, as genuine opposites within the unity of a dialectical action. As Frye states, "there is no division, though there may be a distinction."

My examples, of course, are not random but are intended to reveal the unresolved conflict with the concept of archetype. As a dialectical principle, it describes that flash of recognition which transports the critic beyond himself within the most elemental feeling of the poem, where poet and critic see the world of the poem with the same eyes and touch its objects with the same hands. Frye knows all too well that such recognition cannot be direct, and that certainly literature cannot be taught directly. Yet even in Frye's descriptions of this moment, it is not thereby conceived as an immediacy contained within the mediate development of a dialectic. Literature "is there to serve mankind," a "power to be possessed," and the experience of such a power is incommunicable. Thus it is more like a substance, a first term or goal in a series rather than a moment in a full dialectical action.

Indeed, in *Anatomy* the archetype as the basis for criticism is conceived as original in the sense of a first pattern or model rather than as originative, and this is a classificatory principle. The argument of *Anatomy* proceeds by the either/or categories of "direct experience" and criticism, value-judgments and knowledge, "commentary" (allegory) and criticism (archetypal), making and knowing, existential projection and intrinsic categories. Individual essays are organized in the same way, such as "Theory of Myths" with its division of apocalyptic/demonic imagery. Archetype becomes nothing more than a general category. "Recognition," too, assumes a different meaning. It signifies the critical realization of an identity between any particular work and the total form of literature, the most general pattern criticism can articulate for the shape of literature as a whole.

Cogent criticism of Frye's thinking as a schema of classification is not hard to find. The best examples are William Wimsatt's 1965 English Institute essay and Tzvetan Todorov's first chapter in *The Fantastic*. These are apposite because they reach a remarkably similar conclusion in radically opposed ways. For Wimsatt, Frye's archetypal patterns may indeed represent true patterns: "But in that sense they are also truistic, simplistic, and uninteresting" (*NF*, 93). In order even to pretend to accuracy, they must represent such prodigious abstractions from particular works as to be irrelevant. Frye then simply reimposes these abstract patterns on the text as if he had discovered the deeply originative central form which explains all the detail in the work, as if we could explain *King Lear* by saying that, like all men, Lear was born, and in *x* amount of time died, the ultimate form of the seasonal cycle. The absurdity of such reasoning, says Wimsatt, means that Frye must then decorate these clichés with his "Hallowe'en cast of characters and the mazes of their cyclic action" (*NF*, 96), the result of which may be more specific, but also wildly idiosyncratic, arbitrary, and in fact contradictory in places.

Todorov agrees that Frye provides an arbitrary schema, but he proposes to explain the reason for it in a different way. Frye directly opposes structuralist thought, according to Todorov, by an acceptance of this postulate: "The *structures* formed by literary phenomena *manifest themselves at the level of those phenomena*—i.e. those structures are directly observable" (*F*, 17). Thus while Wimsatt sees Frye as abstracting from the density of a work, Todorov suggests that Frye is operating under the delusion that those structures are not abstractions at all. In the line "Rocks, moss, stonecrop, iron, merds," for example, we are to see the *structure* of demonic imagery rather than the *structure* of apocalyptic imagery in exactly the same way as we see "moss" rather than, say, "dew." Words and imagery exist on the same level as the structure of words and imagery.

For Todorov, the first result is that Frye must forgo the very methodological certainty he seeks to achieve: "One of the words most often encountered in *Anatomy* is surely the word 'often' and its synonyms" (*F*, 18). More seriously, if structure and phenomena exist on the same level, if there is not an "ideal" or "virtual" distance between them, one has no means of elaborating a coherent structure except by arbitrary choice, never knowing whether the object of one's choice was a genuine structure or a local image: "It might even be said that the man who classifies cannot do his job so well: his classification is arbitrary, for it does not rest on an explicit theory—it is a little like those pre-Linnean classifications of living organisms which readily constructed a category of all animals which scratch themselves . . ." (*F*, 19; Todorov's ellipsis)

As devastating as these criticisms are, neither Wimsatt nor Todorov attends to the peculiar status accorded classification in the movement of Frye's thought. For all its grandiose pretensions to scientific detachment and systematic accounting for its theoretical assumptions, *Anatomy* should be read as an act of a human mind and not merely the systematic product of that mind. The problem in *Anatomy* is that it is composed of two incipient and contradictory actions, neither of which is fully realized. The ambiguity is here:

> In looking at a picture, we may stand close to it and analyze the details of brush work and palette knife. This corresponds roughly to the rhetorical analysis of the new critics in literature. At a little distance back, the design comes into clearer view, and we study rather the content represented: this is the best distance for realistic Dutch pictures, for example, where we are in a sense reading the picture. The further back we go, the more conscious we are of the organizing design. At a great distance from, say, a Madonna, we can see nothing but the archetype of the Madonna, a large centripetal blue mass with a contrasting point of interest at its center. In the criticism of literature, too, we often have to "stand back" from the poem to see its archetypal organization (*AC*, 140).

Now for Wimsatt, Frye "backs up" only to abstract patterns from the specificity of the work. The process is analogous to the optical illusion of the "inductive survey" in the "Polemical Introduction" to *Anatomy*, one unfortunately still being repeated as late as *The Critical Path*. Todorov, on the other hand, could understand the procedure as an attempt to gain a perspective on what is actually there in the work, not a generalized shadow merging into all other works. One's perspective will change as he gets closer or moves further away, but the work remains the same, and what we see remains equally "in" the work.

What I want to propose is that the passage I have quoted from *Anatomy* is itself intended to operate as an "ideal" or "virtual" mimesis of the originative recognition which generates the archetype as a dialectical principle. This originative recognition is wordless; the original (the model) mimesis is communicable. The virtual origin of criticism in the process of "backing up" is mimetically identical with an originative "passing into" the work, like a mirror image of it. There is thus to be an omega point, an implicit identity of archetype as originative and archetype as original, and ultimately an identity of dialectical and classificatory thought. The non-arbitrariness of archetypal organization does not derive from an "inductive survey" with all its connotations of nineteenth-century scientism which Wimsatt and Todorov rightly expose. Rather, that "survey" itself is a second-order operation, at once at an absolute remove from the experience of literature and yet mystically at one with it. It is as if Frye would direct criticism to its actual origin, in the sense in which I used the term in my introduction, by projecting the possibility of an identity between the substance of experiencing the "power" of literature and the virtual imitation of that power which is the "objective" structure of literature as a total form.

One wants to say that such a position cannot be criticized effectively; it is an article of faith, to be justified, if at all, by the results it can engender. But that is too easy. The claims Frye makes for his criticism are those of an autodidact, and the consummate arrogance with which he categorizes other critical positions elides any innocuousness of good intentions. R. G. Collingwood has demonstrated convincingly the incompatibility of classificatory and dialectical thought; one is based on substance, the other, at least for Collingwood, on act. In the case of *Anatomy*, an effaced dialectic is no better than none at all. Here is the climactic assertion of identity in the "Theory of Symbols":

> Thus the center of the literary universe is whatever poem we happen to be reading. One step further, and the poem appears as a microcosm of all literature, an individual manifestation of the total order of words. Anagogically, then, the symbol is a monad, all symbols being united in a single infinite and eternal verbal symbol which is, as *dianoia*, the Logos, and, as *mythos*, total creative act (*AC*, 121).

As with biological specimens, each new work becomes nothing more than an immediate manifestation of the class "Literature," and the meaning of "total creative act" is reduced to something like the truism that new frogs get born. Todorov makes the distinction Frye never quite achieves: "Now there is a qualitative difference as to the meanings of the terms 'genre' and 'specimen,' depending on whether they are applied to natural beings or to works of the mind" (F, 5). And a qualitative difference is something which must be articulated as fully as possible and not entrusted to mystical identities. One can only hope that the statement I quoted at the beginning of this discussion is not the end, after all, to "The Road of Excess," for to really believe it would require abandoning a classificatory methodology for good.

III

Structuralism is a philosophy of enunciatory distance. The importance of Saussure and linguistics for a structuralist understanding of literature does not lie so much in the distinction between synchrony and diachrony, although this argument has been advanced impressively by Fredric Jameson in *The Prison-House of Language*, or in the attempt at reintegration in Jakobson or Benveniste. It is rather in the peculiar result of one of Saussure's central insights, that language is a system of differences, a result which transposes "to say" as an act of speech, of *parole*, into an intelligible configurating of acoustic space. This is not to argue that words, like things, are separated *in* space, but almost the reverse. Things, like words, like myths, are intelligible to the extent that they can be seen within a virtual relationship of implicatory differencing. "We shall be concerned here with the death of myths, not in time but in space," runs the opening sentence of a recent essay by Lévi-Strauss.

In the work of Merleau-Ponty, phenomenology was forced to integrate the temporal transformations of the subject into the development of history in a way which precluded both the distanced objectivity that reduced history to a spectacle of processive change and the truism of neo-historicism that man is *in* time. But what if transformation could be conceived spatially rather than temporally? If the essence of transformation was difference as distance rather than difference as process, then would it not be the case that a certain distanced objectivity was not only possible but necessary to describe accurately the object of study? The distinction between synchrony and diachrony is useful as means to an end, an altering of the very notion of transformation itself: "We shall be concerned here with the death of myths, not in time but in space." Such transformation, of space and not of time, is the fundamental subject of structuralist research in the work of Roland Barthes.

Now the concept of an identity at the center of both Hirsch's and Frye's thought elides the necessity to explain, to render intelligible, the movement of transformation itself. Change, movement, contingency is measured against an ideal point of stability, a point where no further change or substitution or transformation is permitted. While Barthes, like Hirsch and Frye, projects the possibility of a "criticism of criticisms" to order the various interpretive "codes" by which a work of literature may be approached, his subject is gathered from what is only shadow in their work, the action of transformation and not the product of it. An identity as product or goal, even a potential one, is a return to substance and its categories, a regression from structuralism to taxonomy. At the same time, Barthes need not implicate the critic in the same way that Gentile must in his actualist aesthetics or Merleau-Ponty in his development of phenomenology. If transformation is a matter of difference as distance, then the critic is obliged to elaborate—to "lose" himself, to distance himself—a virtual structure which remains at a distance from his material.

The importance of difference has not always occupied a central place in Barthes' thought. Even in an interview printed as the last essay in *Critical Essays*, Barthes is arguing that difference is the "motor" only of diachrony and not genuine history. Paradoxically, history is synchronic, an intelligible form that can be exhaustively studied as opposed to the merely temporal process of diachronic change. Yet there has always been implicit in Barthes' work a sense that the synchronic itself is invaded by a doubleness, a "duplicity," which is not so easily characterized. In

"Literature and Metalanguage" (1959) he writes: "And then, probably with the first shocks to the good conscience of the bourgeoisie, literature began to regard itself as double: at once object and scrutiny of that object, utterance and utterance of that utterance, literature object and metaliterature" (*CE*, 97). In a much later essay in *Critical Essays*, Barthes elaborates the consequences of this doubleness for the critic:

> . . . simultaneously an insistent proposition of meaning and a stubbornly fugitive meaning, literature is indeed only a *language*, i.e. a system of signs; its being is not in its message but in this "system." And thereby the critic is not responsible for reconstructing the work's message but only its system, just as the linguist is not responsible for deciphering the sentence's meaning but for establishing the formal structure which permits this meaning to be transmitted. It is by acknowledging itself as no more than a language (or more precisely, a metalanguage) that criticism can be—paradoxically but authentically—both objective and subjective, historical and existential, totalitarian and liberal (*CE*, 259-60).

Literature is only a language, but in a way that accentuates the doubleness of language rather than projecting a more clearly manifest synchronic form. The difficulty in studying literature is not a difficulty in deciphering a *message*, in accounting for a sequence of signs and what those signs signify, but in accounting for the duplicity of the *system* formed by the sign sequence. Difference as distancing, as a simultaneous tracing and effacing of meaning, has become the "motor" not of diachrony, but of a synchronic system itself.

The language-system of a text has a content which can be perceived consecutively or diachronically, something like what Frye posits in "Myth, Fiction, and Displacement" as the "power of continuity" which keeps us reading until the end. Frye, however, moves immediately to the organization of literature as a total form and then to the recognition of an identity between the particular work and the total form once the critic has "frozen" the work to examine its parts as a simultaneous presence, a synchronic system. Barthes, on the other hand, argues that the system of a particular text as a whole is itself a signifier which has as its signified another kind of "content," an insistence that it is literature *of a particular kind*. Thus this signified becomes in its turn another sign-system which at once signifies a system of literature even as it effaces that insistence by stubbonly refusing to be subsumed into it.

Barthes' *S/Z*, a "commentary" on Balzac's story "Sarrasine," shows the extent to which Barthes is willing to push his understanding of the double functioning of a language-system. "Sarrasine" is a frame story, told by a narrator in order to seduce a listener, much as Balzac can be seen as "seducing" the reader into an acceptance of the "realistic" credibility of his story by the device of the frame. In the story told by the narrator, the artist, Sarrasine, is intent on consummating his desire with Zambinella, a *castrato* opera singer whom Sarrasine through most of the story thinks a woman. When he discovers Zambinella's true identity, he attempts to destroy the statue he had made of him/her. But the story ends in catastrophe, the "message" of the statue having been the loss of a desired object, Zambinella, just as the creation of the statue has been made possible by Sarrasine's "embrace" of castration. Within the frame, narrator and listener then take leave of each other, their physical desire unconsummated except in the ambiguity of the system of the frame signifying as a message the duplicitous system of creation/castration in the story, itself signifying as a message the system of Sarrasine's statue, in turn signifying a *lost* message, a *lost* object of desire. Through his elaboration of the five "codes" by which "Sarrasine" can be approached, Barthes would read the text of the Balzac story into the text of all literature, as he reads the transformational structure of the story into the reader, who must be "divided into two subjects, into two cultures, into two languages, *into two hearing-spaces*" (*S/Z*, 150; italics mine). The loss of nuclear self becomes the necessary distance to constitute the reader's understanding of "Sarrasine."

We are now in a position to understand the fullest sense in which a critical metalanguage is paradoxical, in the way first suggested in *Critical Essays*, as "both objective and subjective, historical and existential, totalitarian and liberal." The critic is required to demonstrate exhaustively the language-system of the text, to "saturate" it as fully as possible by transforming it into the language-object of his own metalanguage. He is not free to choose this incident or this symbol as containing *the* meaning. Thus his work is objective and totalitarian. Yet he must also recognize that the text is never a "simple" language-object, that it, too, is a system which signifies another object. In exposing this distance within the text itself, the critic invariably exposes the distance between his metalanguage and the language of the text;

he destroys his own metalanguage even as he elaborates it. His work can represent only a "suspended objectivity," a virtual totality which must always liberally admit other possibilities, even its own supersession. Thus, paradoxically, it is only by maintaining and recognizing a certain distance between himself and the text that he can be said to have been in any way complete. "Completeness" means not interiority or a self-contained system but rather to be implicated in the distancing of transformation. A "criticism of criticisms" henceforth must be the "process"—my quotation marks are to indicate that such process is spatial and not temporal—of transformation rather than an attempt at determining an immediate identity, or even the stability of a synchronic system.

The peculiarly regressive structure entailed is clearest in this remarkable concluding passage to *Système de la mode*, a passage which Fredric Jameson in *The Prison-House of Language* uses as a means of marking his most damaging criticism of structuralism:

> It is a relation [between the "system-object" of the text and the metalanguage of the critic] which is at once transitory [*éphémère*] and necessary, because human knowledge can participate in the becoming of the world only through a series of successive metalanguages, each one of which is alienated in the instant that determines it. This dialectic again can be expressed in formal terms: in speaking of the rhetorical signified in his own metalanguage, the analyst inaugurates (or reassumes) an infinite science: for should it happen for someone (another, or himself later on) to undertake an analysis of his writing and to attempt to reveal its latent content, it would be necessary for this someone to have recourse to a new metalanguage, which would in his turn expose him: a day will inevitably come when structural analysis will pass to the rank of a language-object and be absorbed into a superior system that will explain it in turn. This infinite construction is not sophisticated: it accounts for the transitory and, as it were, suspended objectivity of research and confirms what might be called the Heracleitean characteristics of human knowledge, at every point when by its object it is condemned to fuse [*confondre*] truth and language. This is a necessity which structuralism precisely tries to understand, that is to say [*de parler*]: the semiologist is he who expresses his future death in the same terms by which he has named and understood the world (*SM*, 293; partially quoted in *PH*, 208, in a slightly different translation).

And here is Jameson's comment on the passage: "Thus synchronic certainty dissolves into the pathos of relativistic historicism: and this because a theory of models cannot recognize itself for a model without undoing the very premises on which it is itself founded" (*PH*, 208). But to accept Jameson's argument immediately is to move too fast.

"This infinite construction is not sophisticated"—it is the exact implication of this statement which must concern us most, for temporal difference has in fact been displaced by spatial distance, and the distinction is significant. Rather than a "pathos," Barthes is holding forth another possibility for an "identity." In his paper delivered at the 1966 Johns Hopkins conference Barthes argues that

> just as temporality, person, and diathesis define the positional field of the subject, so modern literature is trying, through various experiments, to establish a new status in writing for the agent of writing. The meaning or goal of this effort is to substitute the instance of discourse for the instance of reality (or the referent). . . . The field of the writer is nothing but writing itself, not as the pure "form" conceived by an aesthetic of art for art's sake, but, much more radically, as the only area [*espace*] for the one who writes (*LC*, 144; translator's brackets).

A little bit later, he restates the goal of the effort:

> We are all trying, with different methods, styles, perhaps even prejudices, to get to the core of this linguistic pact [*pacte de parole*] which unites the writer and the other, so that—and this is a contradiction which will never be sufficiently pondered—each moment of discourse is both absolutely new and absolutely understood (*LC*, 144; translator's brackets).

There is an identical *space* where what is new and what is understood, the writer and the other, necessity and contingency—all of which make up the infinite construction of distancing—can be understood as somehow at one. If difference is conceived temporally, the differential movement becomes a mark of exclusion, even if the exclusion is hidden in the illusive continuity of the referent sustained by the "realistic" novel. But if, on the other hand, difference is spatial, a transformation, a distancing, each "instance" can be inclusive rather than exclusive. The differential as distance can be part of the very idea of space; it is, in fact, the intelligibility of the idea of the "same" space. While Hirsch and Frye in their different ways could project an identity only by positing an ideal point where difference disappears, Barthes projects an identity as the mutually implicatory distancing everywhere in the act of writing, a "space" of discourse that can be all-inclusive. It is this reasoning which underlies the "absolutely plural text" posited in *S/Z*.

Unlike Frye's total form which is contingent on the lack of difference, the immediate identity between any particular work and the whole of literature, Barthes' ideal text depends upon each individual text as different, existing at a distance from the others. So in the beginning of *S/Z*, he can criticize any attempt to derive "a great narrative structure" that comprehends all texts, because the individual text "thereby loses its difference" (*S/Z*, 9). To insist on the differences of individual texts is to participate in an infinite construction of the identity of all texts within the "instance" of discourse, and one which need not posit an arbitrary and determinate goal that collapses all distance and difference.

The ambiguity in Barthes' work which allows Jameson's critique is that such a possibility does not thereby overcome temporality. In the passage from *Système de la mode*, the ambiguity is even in the use of a phrase such as "a day will inevitably come." An "instance" of discourse as a space, a distancing, implies a simultaneous presence of distances, and distance can be presence only in the presupposition of an unambiguous present, one uncomplicated by the presence of past or future. That is the reason "this infinite construction" must *not* be sophisticated. Returning to *S/Z*, "the division of listeners" is possible because the distance within the listener, the effect of two listeners, is everywhere *present* to constitute this distancing *presence*. Presence is difference as it elides the difference between presence and present.

Here Jameson's critique of Barthes can become as devastating as the critique of Hirsch and Frye that is possible from within Barthes' position. The very act of positing an infinite identity of transformational distance determines the closure of temporality in the present, the result of which is the "relativistic historicism" Jameson finds at the end of *Système de la mode* as each closed, present moment mechanically passes into the next closed present. Every message is a message of loss, because the inclusiveness of a spatial, transformational system signifies always the exclusiveness of the temporal moment in a movement of signification impossible to account for. Rather than the thinking through of an actual origin, transformation as the subject of structuralist research in Barthes is the objectification, the virtual distancing, of the actual by an hypostasis of the temporal moment as a substantial identity.

Thus it is that even in Barthes, who for literary criticism, I think, takes the concept of "virtual" as far as it can go, there remains the impossibility of explaining a most elemental relation. How are difference as temporalization and difference as distancing conjoined? To begin by radically distinguishing them—one exclusive, the other inclusive—is a judgment that can never be accounted for within the closure of the distinction itself. Any methodology inaugurated by a distinction which effaces the insecurity of such judgment at its center is condemned by its very nature to recapitulate the disjunctive origin *ad infinitum*. Barthes seems to me to know this ambiguity so well that to insist any more on the point is a redundancy. What I will insist on is the necessity to re-think our critical traditions in such a way that we do not assume too quickly that we have passed beyond the problems they pose for us, especially in the facile illusion of constructing a critical methodology which is self-regulating, at a virtual distance from the elaboration of an aesthetic and a philosophy. For us, even the actualism of Gentile, were it to enter critical thought as I hope it will, poses a problem rather than a resolution. But that does not seem to me a similiarly hopeless state of affairs.

NOTES

1. The following is a list of works to be cited in this essay, with the abbreviations employed for convenience. I have tried to use English translations of French texts whenever available, but in the case of Barthes' *Système de la mode* and *S/Z* the translations are my own.

Barthes, Roland. *Essais Critiques*. Paris: Seuil, 1964. Trans. by Richard Howard as *Critical Essays*. Evanston: Northwestern University Press, 1972. Abbreviated *CE*.

Système de la mode. Paris: Seuil, 1967. Abbreviated *SM*.

S/Z. Paris: Seuil, 1971. Abbreviated *S/Z*.

"To Write: An Intransitive Verb?" in *The Languages of Criticism and the Sciences of Man*, ed. Richard Macksey and Eugenio Donato. Baltimore: Johns Hopkins University Press, 1970. Abbreviated *LC*.

Frye, Northrop. *Anatomy of Criticism*. New York: Atheneum, 1969. Abbreviated *AC*.

"The Road of Excess," in *The Stubborn Structure*, ed. Max Black. Ithaca: Cornell University Press, 1970. Abbreviated *SS*.

Hirsch, E. D. *Validity in Interpretation*. New Haven: Yale University Press, 1967. Abbreviated VI.

"Three Dimensions of Hermeneutics." *New Literary History*, 2 (Winter, 1972), 245-61. Abbreviated *Three*.

Jameson, Fredric. *The Prison-House of Language*. Princeton: Princeton University Press, 1972. Abbreviated *PH*.

Lévi-Strauss, Claude. *Le Cru et le cuit*. Paris: Plon, 1964. Trans. by John and Doreen Weightman as *The Raw and the Cooked*. New York: Harper and Row, 1969. Abbreviated *RC*.

Todorov, Tzvetan. *Introduction à la littérature fantastique*. Paris: Seuil, 1969. Trans. by Richard Howard as *The Fantastic*. Cleveland: Case Western Reserve University Press, 1973. Abbreviated *F*.

Wimsatt, William. "Northrop Frye: Criticism as Myth," in *Northrop Frye in Modern Criticism*, ed. Murray Krieger. New York: Columbia University Press, 1966. Abbreviated *NF*.

2. See especially Benedetto Croce, *Nuovi saggi di estetica*, 3rd ed. (Bari: Laterza, 1948); and Giovanni Gentile, *La filosofia dell'arte*, 2nd ed. (Firenze: Sansoni, 1950), trans. by Giovanni Gullace as *The Philosophy of Art* (Ithaca: Cornell University Press, 1972).

STRUCTURALISM AND THE READING OF CONTEMPORARY FICTION

R. E. JOHNSON

EVEN THE MOST SUMMARY READING of structuralist materials will discover sometimes portentous claims for their efficacy in divers activities, not the least of which is literary criticism. It is certainly not my purpose to dispute these claims. But I would prefer the more modest assertion that the ideas of certain structuralists (who may or may not be willing to accept their being so classified) can help us arrive at non-linear, even non-spatial, working definitions of form which are especially functional in the reading of modern literature. This modicum seems to me sufficient justification for a serious appraisal of what these thinkers are saying. They may save us from too quickly categorizing, and hence dismissing because our categories have been too limited, something in which we might otherwise have found pleasure and significance—albeit, perhaps, of different kinds and in different ways.

In line with this conviction, I will attempt to supplement the discussions elsewhere in this issue with a general review of some structuralist assumptions that seem to me to have a bearing on contemporary fiction. Somewhat simplistic and necessarily incomplete, this survey should, however, provide sufficient grounding for the latter part of the essay: an application of these ideas, rather than of a specific methodology, to three contemporary American writers—William H. Gass, Donald Barthelme, and Robert Coover.

Mr. Johnson received his doctorate from the State University of New York at Buffalo and is at present teaching American literature and modern fiction at Augusta College, Augusta, Georgia.

As the structuralist sees it, language doesn't describe the "real" world (this is a practically impossible task). Rather it inscribes the functioning of consciousness. The structuralist literary critic sees language as literature's world—its subject and formal paradigmatic model—as well as its material. Thus in literature we are dealing with something which denies its own authority (transcendence) and purpose (intersubjective communication) while it asserts them. The sign serves to distance the other from the signified and signifier while it "tells" him about itself. It simultaneously subverts the teller in his pretense to know his subject. Consequently literature both is charged with meaning and yet denies understanding in any total or complete sense.

The work of the critic is both unique and forever derivative. He is inextricably bound to his text, which he merely repeats; yet that repetition, like any repetition, involves difference as well as sameness. In this sense the critic's job is to himself "articulate" the text, make the material his own by "carving out" his reading from all others. The literary author, in turn, is not the unreflecting speaker; he is the speaker about the speaker. Consequently he gets as close to the "subject" of his work as the linguist does to the (disappearing) signified. Criticism is thus at one more remove from the original signified. The original signified, however, is itself a signifier, the subject an interpretation of another subject.

Therefore the critic cannot deal with the real subject or with the writer's subject but only with the writer *as* subject—the relationship between the writer and the literary structures through which he is constituted. Of course, the critic is himself a writer and thus becomes subject to the same sort of critique. In fact, his language self-reflexively initiates the critique even as did his poet's or his novelist's "before" him.

The critic's method, then, has as its ground of being (or non-being) a critique of his own position, which self-critique he assumes in his author as well. His focus is on the writer as Dr. Jekyll and Mr. Hyde, on the relations between the writer and himself, the writer and his self-constituting and self-destructing structures. His task is a repetition or articulation of the work under study, all the while mediating between the (illusory) loss of self in sameness or total identification of reader with author and the (illusory) objective detachment of the scientific explicator. His goal is simultaneously to recover and destroy the writer's model—those structures of inter-alterity by means of which the writer writes himself—by a synchronic display of the acts of structuration (signification) that occur in a given body of literature.

Such concerns might lead the structuralist reader to ask some of the following questions, among others, of a particular work or set of works:

1. To what system does the pivotal language belong, i.e., what system of stasis or exchange is metaphorically rendered in the dominant language? What sort of structural patterns and relationships emerge from the repetition and interplay of these terms?

2. If there is ambivalence in the major terms, how does it function?

3. What sort of structural similarities/antinomies can be discovered/generated from the linguistic ambivalences?

4. How do the structural relations discovered in questions 1 and 2 propel/abort the movement of the work?

5. What factors complicate the basic structure(s) of the work?

6. How do the inventory of other relationships (linguistic, plot, character, etc.) reflect the paradigmatic structure? (How can they be *translated* into its terminology, equations, etc.?) How does this basic structure and the variations on it explain the otherwise inexplicable (referring here not to meaning, as such, but to function)?

7. In what way can purposeful contradictions/violations of the structure be reappropriated by the consciousness of the author in the work? In what way(s) can they not? (How do they call their own validity into question?)

8. How does the basic structure(s) govern the architecture of the whole (as opposed to the architecture of the part questioned in number 6)?

9. To what degree do these structures reflect the structures in the canon as a whole?

10. To what degree do these structures reflect the structures of an age or era?

11. In what way do these structures call into question the particular critic's enterprise—the critical enterprise as a whole?

The role of the particular imagination incarnated in language in William H. Gass's fiction is effectively to deconstruct the outside world. But this is not to lend support to the view that Gass is a solipsist,[1] at least not in the simplistic sense of that noun. Gass has merely reflected, in the rhythms of his structures, the rhythms of all language and, in fact, of all human activity which is figured in language. His fictions call attention to themselves as real beyond the language which presents them and which they dwarf; and, at the same time, they mock that reality by showing that its beginning and end lie in linguistic forms on which it merely performs variations.

The first story in Gass's collection *In the Heart of the Heart of the Country and Other Stories* apparently takes place at the height of winter in one of the northern middle-western states. Big Hans, a live-in worker on the Segren farm, discovers a neighbor boy lying nearly frozen to death next to their corn crib. Hans and Mrs. Segren try to revive the boy with the reluctant help of the story's narrator, Jorge. When the Pederson kid partially regains consciousness he tells Hans that his home has been taken over by a man in yellow gloves and a green mackinaw who has forced his family at gun-point down into the fruit cellar. Along with Mr. Segren, who has been unwillingly roused from a drunken sleep by his son, Jorge and Hans talk about the plausibility of the story. Provoked by his wife's discovery of one of his hidden whiskey bottles and by Hans' attempt to drink from it, Pa decides that they will go over to the Pederson place.

On the way the sled horse gets stuck and, in the process of getting him disengaged, a runner is broken and Pa loses his liquor bottle. Outside the Pederson house they discover a strange horse frozen in the snow. There is more debate about whether to go or to stay and how to reach the house without being seen. Driven nearly berserk by the cold and snow, Jorge threatens to shoot Pa and Hans, but Pa takes the gun away. Hans and Pa begin to tunnel toward the house until Jorge suggests that perhaps they will find the stranger frozen in the snow next to the dead horse. This proves to be untrue, and, out of vexed frustration, Hans recommits himself to staying just when they seem on the point of returning home.

In the third part of the story Jorge breaks for the house. When he gets there with no mishap, he proudly signals all clear. His father moves out in the open to join Jorge and is immediately shot to death by someone from within the house. Jorge breaks a window and crawls into the basement. He finds no one there and his mind begins to wander from fear and weariness. Finally he hears an upstairs door slam and sees a man riding away. The fire he soon makes in the Pederson kitchen recalls certain of his own summertime experiences, the coming of Hans to the farm, their friendship and rupture. His mind continues to eddy about his family, the Pedersons, the man with the yellow gloves, until finally it settles in on a physical and emotional sense of warmth and freedom.

"The Pederson Kid" contains a number of intermingling processes of exchange, each of which involves traversing a figurative or literal distance. Perhaps the principal exchange is of an objectified and brutalized human world for a subjectivized "natural" world, a fallen world for a prelapsarian existence. Related to this basic exchange is a trade of warmth for cold, Jorge for the Pederson Kid, time for space, the imagined for the real.

The objectivity of the human world is reflected in the monotonous, almost staccato language of the early part of the story (when Jorge's consciousness is largely controlled by Pa's and Hans'), the unemotional prose treatment of material which should, or could, have a great deal of emotional impact. When emotions do appear they are divorced of their heat, spatialized, even put into economic terms.

> He was awful angry because he'd thought ma was going to do something big, something heroic even, especially for her—I know him . . . I know him . . . we felt the same sometimes—while ma wasn't thinking about that at all, not anything like that. There was no way of getting even. It wasn't like getting cheated at the fair. They were always trying, so you got to expect it. Now Hans had given ma something of his—we both had and when we thought she was going straight to Pa—something valuable, a piece of better feeling; but since she didn't know we'd given it to her, there was no easy way of getting it back.[2]

This impression is strengthened by the frequent descriptions that make it appear that things are happening without human intervention (e.g., "the kettle filled") and by the total lack of quotation marks, except for two sentences attributed to the Pederson kid. When perceptions are given in print there appears to be no orderly flow of consciousness; such perceptions are given like a list: "I couldn't be sure he was still asleep. He was a cagey sonofabitch. He'd heard his name. I shook him a little harder and made some noise. Pap-pap-pap-hey, I said" (4). There are no discriminations here between thought, observation, a remark based on past experience, a noise, and a perspective on the self acting and talking. In the schema of the story they are all the same, all merely words. Significance is forced into a hierarchy. We begin with linguistic objects, separated by differing amounts of (typographical) space; first and foremost there is the conjunction of words into significant units and only secondarily, if at all, do the units refer to or evoke some sensory experience. "Just his back. The green mackinaw. The black stocking cap. The yellow gloves. The gun" (14).

The terms in which the human world is presented are unappealing at best, profane, vindictive, frequently scatological at worst.[3] Paradoxically the human world is seen as inhuman, either brutalized by metaphors from the animal world or mechanized by comparison with machines (23). On the other hand, an impressionistic naturalized (rather than natural) world comes increasingly to the fore as Jorge's imagination is given freer rein and his command of the situation grows. We move from a situation where Pa's influence subdues nature[4] to one where Jorge allows his imagination to dovetail with nature, as it were.

> Flakes began to slide out of the sky and rub their corners off on the pane before they were caught by the wind again and blown away. In the gray I couldn't see them. Then they would come—suddenly—from it, like chaff from grain, and brush the window while the wind eddied. Something black was bobbing. It was deep in the gray where the snow was. It bounced queerly and then it went. The black stocking cap, I thought.
>
> . . . . .
>
> Once, when dust rolled up from the road and the fields were high with heavy-handled wheat and the leaves of every tree were gray and curled up and hung head down, I went in the meadow with an old broom like a gun, where the dandelions had begun to seed and the low ground was cracked, and I flushed grasshoppers from the goldenrod in whirring clouds like quail and shot them down. I smelled wheat in the warm wind and every weed. . . . My horse had a golden tail. Dust rolled up behind me. Pa was on the tractor in a broad-brimmed hat. With a fist like a pistol butt and trigger, going fast, I shot him down. (68-69)

This idyll, however, is weighted by the murder(s). Similarly, as the exchange of worlds is about to be completed, we are given the story's version of the fall, the "origin" of the present situation. "It was a night like this one. The wind was blowing hard and the snow was coming hard and I'd built a fire and was sitting by it, dreaming. Ma came and sat near me, and then pa came, burning inside himself, while Hans stayed in the kitchen. All I heard was the fire, and in the fire I saw ma's sad quiet face the whole evening without turning, and I heard pa drinking, and nobody not even me said anything the whole long evening. The next morning Hans went to wake pa and pa threw the pot and Hans got the ax and pa laughed fit to shake the house. It wasn't long before Hans and I took to hating one another and hunting pa's bottles alone" (71). There is no original condition, merely repetition. In Eden the Fall bloomed. At the center of the Fall was the "dream" of Eden. Each bears the other, its succession by the other, and its succession of the other within itself. "First" is an illusion.

It is easy to see how the exchange of coldness for warmth complements the trade of worlds. For Jorge, imagination and the journey out of, and back to, imagination are both in syncopation with his relative degree of warmth. Warmth is associated by Jorge not only with a past edenic condition but also with the veritable paradise which he is given by the story's exchange structures.[5] Warmth and cold, however, are also given ambivalent values. Pa is frequently described as "red" or "burning." And, paradoxically, as Jorge moves toward warmth, the cold takes on a different character. "It was good to be warm but I didn't feel so set against the weather as I had been. I thought I'd like winter pretty well from now on" (72).

The reverse side of the trade-off of worlds is the basic swap of Jorge for the Pederson kid. Jorge intuitively senses the impending exchange, but, at first, he defends himself against it by rejecting the other boy. "He [Pa] didn't give a damn about the Pederson kid, any more than I did. Pederson's kid was just a kid. He didn't carry any weight. Not like I did" (3). The Pederson kid is seen both as absence and as a disturbing presence to Jorge, an item for consumption (he is compared to a chicken "being fixed for the table"), a standard for (negative) comparison, a hollow mark in the snow and his mother's biscuit dough. He has no particular existence for Jorge; he is known only by his outline, against which Jorge defines himself.

But bit by bit Jorge is drawn both to an identification with the kid and to the terrifying conclusion that he seemed to have simply materialized out of the white nothingness. Big Hans forces the identification by inserting Jorge into the place of the kid in his retelling of what went on when the man in yellow gloves invaded the Pederson household (19). On the surface the two families balance. But the Pedersons seem to be the negatives of the Segrens. The former family includes a father who is Pa's exact opposite, a mother who is seen by Jorge as a sex-object (if he's sure she's dead, he wants to sneak a look at her "crotch"), another member called Little Hans and, of course, Stevie, the "Pederson Kid." The latter says nothing (though he is once quoted and is the ostensible subject of the story). By contrast Jorge does all the talking, creates himself *ex nihilo*, out of language, and thus *becomes* the subject.

Finally Jorge is driven out of himself and into the place of the Pederson kid, a place which is both located by the minimal boundaries given by the words "the Pederson kid" and yet a place which is without location. Jorge has been swallowed by the same cold emptiness out of which the boy emerged. "But I stayed where I was, so cold I seemed apart from myself, and wondered if everything had been working to get me in this cellar as a trade for the kid he'd missed. . . . The Pederson kid—maybe he'd been a message of some sort. No, I liked better the idea that we'd been prisoners exchanged. I was back in my own country. No, it was more like I'd been given a country. A new blank land. More and more, while we'd been coming, I'd been slipping out of myself, pushed out by the cold maybe" (62-63).

Jorge first sees the exchange as a kind of murder, a murder which we see him imaginatively performing again and again. He must pay for the exchange of positions. "The kid for killing his family must freeze" (66). (The sentence is purposefully ambiguous and implicates both the Pederson kid and Jorge.) But he gets over this guilt—if we choose to call it that—as he grows in confidence, sense of purpose, and the imaginative range and power to realize this consciousness in language. The killer—the author I would presume, the one faceless alien in this almost perfectly balanced and named world—flees, not inexplicably, but only when Jorge is able to drive him out because his language is increasingly capable of mastery of the situation.[6]

With the departure of "yellow gloves" the victory, the acceptance of the exchange, is settled but not accomplished. Jorge still must extricate himself from the past bound within his memory. His acceptance is sealed in the story's last paragraph. "I had been the brave one and now I was free. The snow would keep me. . . . The way that fellow had come so mysteriously through the snow and done us [Jorge and the Pederson kid] such a glorious turn—well it made me think how I was told to feel in church. The winter time had finally got them all and I really did hope that the kid was as warm as I was now, warm inside and out, burning up, inside and out, with joy" (78-79).

Another, somewhat more abstract, reflection of the basic model can be seen in the exchange of time for space, the nominalization of time. The time that passes in the story is not human time; it is typographical time. There is not a pause between speeches made by characters in a drama, there is a gap in the sequence of print. Yet it is clear that the spaces do appear where there *would be* a pause in conversation or perception. Thinking, or reflection, appears to go on in the blank spaces: "By now the kid was naked.   I was satisfied mine was bigger" (2). What is also clear, however, is that the reflection is *a posteriori* rather than *a priori*: that is, the thinking or reflection is generated by the opposition of the two sentences rather than vice-versa (or rather than there being this sequence: first sentence —thinking—second sentence). Thus time is effectively spatialized. The time of the sentences is the synchronic time of the blank space, which absorbs the diachrony—the "past" of the first sentence, before the thinking existed, and the future time of the second sentence which follows from the thinking—to which the first and second sentences necessarily submitted themselves in becoming language.

In this sense, the blizzard serves as a metaphor for the time-context in which language comes into being. "In a blizzard you got to be where you're going if you're going to get there" (16). A blizzard is an accurate reflection of the chaos of tenses in certain of the passages where Jorge gives his consciousness more or less free rein in imagining future-past-perfect situations. In one, for example, he imagines having found the thawed kid in the spring; in another, some fifty-eight pages later, he imagines the end of "yellow gloves," which, in turn, overlaps the end of the kid.[7] These passages indicate at the very least that the time of consciousness is a time which keeps all times/tenses in their irreducible identity and yet reduces all of them to its own present. Furthermore, the reflection of the one passage near the end of the story by the other near the beginning has the same effect. The stories are different—the dying persons are different—yet they are the same; in both cases the dying person is Jorge. There is in this sense no progress from page fourteen to page seventy-two. There is no point to progress from or to; there is only consciousness and the repetition of its patterns.

When the system is completed, when language and imagination, inextricably in tandem, have done their work, all that is objectionable in Jorge's world, all that is not-Jorge, has been eliminated. He is left with what he has won, imaginatively and linguistically. But this remainder is like a minus figure in mathematics: it has a conceptual but no substantial reality. He has attained a degree of transcendence which is mocked by the fact that there is nothing to transcend.

> The road was gone. Fences, bushes, old machinery: what there might be in any yard was all gone under snow. . . . He'd gone off this way yet there was nothing now to show he'd gone; nothing like a bump of black in a trough or an arm or leg sticking out of the side of a bank like a branch had blown down or a horse's head uncovered like a rock; nowhere Pederson's fences had kept bare he might be lying huddled with the horse on its haunches by him; nothing even the shadows shrinking while I watched to take for something hard and not of snow and once alive. (77-78)

The "story" has been Jorge's generation of himself by fits and starts, by cutting himself off from everything else in the world at the same time he gave meaning to it in the telling.[8] Jorge is, at the end of the story, both the liberated and the isolated word. In Part I it is Pa's action that is determinative of where the story will go in Part II; in Part II it is Hans' action; in Part III it is Jorge's action which is determinative of where the story will go in Parts I and II and III.

It turns out that the Pederson family is not in the fruit cellar. This serves not only to undercut the various stories—the Pederson kid's, Hans', Jorge's—but to make it appear that "yellow gloves" is only created when he is needed. The story is something both given to Jorge and something he makes. In one sense he takes over from Pa and Hans as movers and "yellow gloves" as counter-mover; but in other figurative *and* literal sense (if we look at the story synchronically) he has moved the story from the beginning. His language has been in control; yet there has been an obvious development in the range and versatility of his language and thus of his consciousness.

Jorge's phrasing often recalls that of Huck Finn; and, in a way, he achieves the freedom Huck went off the pages of his novel looking for. But Jorge achieves this freedom only in the role of the Mysterious Stranger, the articulated dream dreamed by a dream. Barthelme's negative lists call to mind everything not on the lists—the whole universe of possibilities. Jorge's naming leaves nothing left; it is naming as shooting, the word-maker as murderer. Yet the dreadful irony is that he must resurrect Pa, have him there to say "Funny, I don't feel nothing" when shot, in order for Jorge to have any identity as murderer or word-maker. If Pa is finally dead, so is Jorge. Hence the necessity of the story, the necessity of "yellow gloves" and Pa and Hans and Ma. As each system of exchange comes equipped with that which calls its value into question or turns its meaning around, so the language of the story comes equipped with that which mocks or subverts its very action by means of *reductio ad absurdum*, alliteration or punning, obvious inconsistencies in the text, foreshadowings which turn out to be both true and untrue, and so on. The "action" of the words thus reflects the action of the characters, theme, setting. . . . And all of the words of the story are positive and negative reflections/generations of the word "Jorge" which is itself, as we have seen, only a center for the infinite exchange of presence and absence.

> Why does language subvert me, subvert my seniority, my medals, my oldness, whenever it gets a chance? What does language have against me—me that has been good to it, respecting its little peculiarities and nicilosities, for sixty years. . . . What do "years" have against me?
>
> Strings of language extend in every direction to bind the world into a rushing, ribald whole.[9]

In these sequences, two Donald Barthelme characters articulate the opposite proclivities of language. These contrary tendencies are responsible not only for the difficulty we have reading Barthelme, but for the difficulty we have reading anyone. Contrary to what James Dickey assumes, Barthelme does not set for himself the goal of accumulating "cute trash." Nor are his "juxtapositions and associations" as "unmotivated" as the basically more sympathetic Tony Tanner finds them.[10] But everywhere he turns Barthelme encounters this opposition in language. The consequent role of his fiction is to act out the almost endless variation on such a problematic.

This vocation could produce a tedious redundancy instead of often bewildering novelty. Barthelme's acts of "repetition," however, correspond in form to those characteristic of certain structuralists. "Repetition is a temporal process that assumes difference as well as resemblance. It functions as a regulative principle of rigor but asserts the impossibility of rigorous identity, etc. Precisely to the extent that all interpretation has to be repetition it also has to be immanent."[11]

The grounds for such a definition are offered by "The Catechist," a story in Barthelme's last-published collection, *Sadness*. In this narrative one priest is being catechised by another priest. The process is marked not only by the fact that the catechist reads aloud the instructions (instead of the words of the catechism) but also by the fact that he inserts various bits of apparently irrelevant information and employs various visual aids, ridiculous in the particular context of the story. Several times over the course of the account, the catechumen, who is also the narrator, observes: "We have this conversation every day. No detail changes" (*S*, 121).

The two characters are unable to escape their limiting context. Everything in the story is part of the catechism and the catechism is all there is. One might find the story a piece of social satire aimed at Catholicism. Within this frame, the fact that the story is just one enactment of an experience which repeats itself *ad infinitum* merely reinforces our sense of the restrictiveness of the priest's position. He has no freedom, to marry, say, or to think for himself. The catechists' questions and actions as well as the catechumen's answers, in being continually repeated, are divested of any significance except as ritual. This is another mirror of how the Catholic's vitality is subdued by the regimen of traditional dogma and practice.

But such an approach does not get us very far; it is subverted as quickly (but as ambiguously) as the complaining character in our first Barthelme quotation. The story provides us with a model of the writer's necessary relationship with his language, of the reader's relationship with a text. What is true of this text is true of any: in diachronic time the story develops; the sometimes absurd actions of the catechist are surprising; the questions demand answers; at any point the situation can go a number of ways depending on what the characters do. The resemblance of the story to a catechism is inverted by its surprising turns, not only the actions of the catechist but also the affirmation of the catechumen that "There is no day on which this conversation is not held and no detail of this conversation which is not replicated on any particular day on which the conversation is held" (*S*, 126). Diachronically, ritual is always new as it is articulated by a different person (different, even, from himself yesterday), at a different time, in different tones. On the other hand, considered synchronically, the story is always over before it began. What one has are not new situations, but more of the same. Language provides the finite limits within which, and against which, the writer may write and the reader may read.

Yet this text doesn't just begin with the first word and end with the last word—or vice versa. Like any Barthelme story, this one self-consciously begins and ends an infinite number of times *in the middle*.[12] "I gave his face some additional looks," one of the dwarfs in *Snow White* says (*SW*, 154). When one gives up the flow of perception described by the statement, "I looked at his face," or, "I was looking at his face," there is no stopping the fragmentation of perception. There is no such thing as a whole "look," only the process of looking fragmented into minutes, seconds, milliseconds and so on. No wonder one narrator says that "fragments are the only forms I trust" (*UPUA*, 157).[13] Here, in the middle, as it were, is room for "development":[14] in the letter as it both joins and repels other letters, in the word, the sentence, the paragraph, the story, the theme, the characters as they do similarly. One must conclude that the story, language itself, like the catechist's "analysis," is both "terminable and interminable" (*S*, 125); and, consequently, it is both always new and never new.

The paradigmatic situation in Barthelme's fiction presents a basic incongruity between the way something supposedly is and the way it is viewed, or between different ways of viewing the same thing. Typically, Barthelme complicates matters so that the incongruity both is and is not real. A clear example is the early story "Me and Miss Mandible." "Miss Mandible wants to make love to me but she hesitates because I am officially a child; I am, according to the records, according to the gradebook on her desk, according to the card index in the principal's office, eleven years old. There is a misconception here, one that I haven't quite managed to get cleared up yet. I am in fact thirty-five . . ." (*CBDC*, 97) The narrator finds himself fairly well prepared for his unusual situation because he was formerly an insurance adjuster, a person herein defined as one who has the double vision to see something not only as it is but as it is deconstructed (*CBDC*, 98-99). Responsible for his situation, that of Miss Mandible, Sue Ann Brownly (who recalls his wife in his former "life-role") and the others in the class is "the game." At the center of the game is not rule or authority but a question mark, the game or play itself, referred to in the story as "(Who decides?)."[15]

Life is defined as such a game, the pointless and inconsistent rules of which are to be read out of the game only after it has been played; but, paradoxically, part of playing is the pretense/assumption that such "rules" pre-exist the game. "(Who decides?)" evolves whole systems of math, science, and history which promise that reality is knowable if one will only discover and apply the right formulae. Such promises confuse and upset the narrator who consequently disputes them. But then the narrator is obviously out of touch with any reality at all; hence his easy exchange of "life-roles."

The formulae generated by "(Who decides?)" are for the purposes of making process relevant (an obvious contradiction, doomed at the start by the conflict of its ground and goal, if by nothing else). The name of this activity is Interpretation. Interpretation is taking a system of signs, from it generating another, and then pretending that there is a meaningful, even causal, connection between the two. From one of Miss Mandible's books, entitled *Making the Processes Meaningful*, he reads an injunction to apply the processes to "life-like problems" (*CBDC*, 101). In the very next paragraph the narrator proceeds to show that this is precisely what he himself is doing (i.e., making the processes meaningful) by taking a sentence out of the context of the book and then generating his own interpretation. The point here seems to be that all narratives are interpretations in this sense, are necessarily out of context. To tell a story is therefore to submit oneself to "(Who decides?)," the centerless center. "For an instant I am on the brink of telling her my story. Something, however, warns me not to attempt it. Here I am safe, I have a place; I do not wish to entrust myself once more to the whimsy of authority" (*CBDC*, 107).

The action in the classroom offers us a paradigm for the process of Interpretation. "Amos Darin has been found drawing a dirty picture in the cloakroom. Sad and inaccurate, it was offered not as a sign of something else, but as an act of love in itself. It has excited even those who have not seen it, even those who saw but understood only that it was dirty. . . . From time to time Miss Mandible looks at me reproachfully, as if blaming me for the uproar. But I did not create this atmosphere, I am caught in it like all the others" (107). The spiral begins with the sign as act, followed by the interpretation of the sign without understanding and the interpretations of this interpretation, the interpretation practiced by the narrator and Miss Mandible when they do the "real thing" in the cloakroom, the interpretation of their act by Sue Ann Brownly and the authorities, and so on.

The narrator rightly perceives that this generation of signs/interpretations involves "interpersonal relations" in all possible forms. To the degree that they are caught in its spiral, such relations are determined by it or at least reflective of it. The generation process is certainly not limited to abstract systems such as math or language, narrowly defined (the narrator quickly realizes this; see page 106). In fact the principal "model" for linguistic and other forms of action in the story is the triangular relationship between Debbie, Eddie, and Liz. This (ultimately unknowable) relationship not only has generated eighteen stories in eighteen copies of *Movie–TV Secrets* but it also generates the classroom atmosphere, itself the ultimate source of Amos Darin's drawing. In short, a derived sign is the origin of the original sign.

> Who are these people, Debbie, Eddie, Liz, and how did they get themselves in such a terrible predicament? Sue Ann knows, I am sure; it is obvious that she has been studying their history as a guide to what she may expect when she is suddenly freed from this drab, flat classroom.
>
> I am angry and I shove the magazines back at her with not even a whisper of thanks.
>
> . . . Sue Ann is absent; I suspect that yesterday's *exchange* has driven her to her bed. Guilt hangs about me. She is not responsible, I know, for what she reads, for the *models* proposed to her by a venal publishing industry. . .
>
> . . . . . .
>
> Sue Ann Brownly caught Miss Mandible and me in the cloakroom, during recess, and immediately threw a fit. . . . She ran out of the

room weeping, straight for the principal's office, certain now which of us was Debbie, which Eddie, which Liz. (*CBDC*, 106, 110—emphasis mine)

The narrator's principal work as a student is in demythologizing "all of the mysteries that perplexed me as an adult" (*CBDC*, 109). "The great discovery of my time here" is the arbitrariness of the sign. "We read signs as promises . . . but I say, looking around me in this incubator of future citizens, that signs are signs, and that some of them are lies" (*CBDC*, 109). What makes the sign truly arbitrary is that just "some" of them are lies. Some of them, Miss Mandible's interpretations of the signs generated by the narrator, for example, are true, are fulfilled.[16] Some, like Brenda's interpretation of these same signs, remain unfulfilled. Signs are erratic and unpredictable; hence the fallacy of seeing them as anything but arbitrary.

Perhaps because of their arbitrary nature, or at least in tandem with it, signs have no given hierarchy of value, only an assigned value. One may "cut out" a sign at any level, or, more accurately, one may focus on the cutting out achieved by a particular sign and follow its rippling work infinitely inward or outward, infinitely upward or downward. The value of the place one chooses to start is purely relative to the act of focusing. This is indicated by two items from *Movie-TV Secrets*. The first is an "exclusive picture" which the magazine says "isn't what it seems. We know what the gossipers will do. So in the interests of a nice guy, we're publishing the facts first" (*CBDC*, 105). Here we "begin" with the picture, itself an interpretation of. . . . Then we have the (imagined) interpretation of the picture by "gossipers." This interpretation is, of course, the sign behind the picture, the sign which the picture is supposed to be duplicating. But then there is also another level of interpretation which is vying for this primary status, the sign called by the magazine the "facts." The interpretation by the narrator is essentially the same as the interpretation by the gossipers: "divorce evidence." This sign, obviously the one informing the picture and hence the "original" sign, is but another transformation of Debbie, Eddie, Liz.

The second item is an advertisement. "What do these hipless eleven-year-olds think when they come across, in the same magazine, the full-page ad for Maurice de Paree, which features 'Hip Helpers' or what appear to be padded rumps? ('A real undercover agent that adds appeal to those hips and derriere, both!') If they cannot decipher the language the illustrations leave nothing to the imagination. 'Drive him frantic. . .' the copy continues" (*CBDC*, 105). This series of significations also appears to follow the picture—interpretation—facts sequence. Or perhaps it reverses the sequence since the text, our text, presents the facts—padded rumps——followed by the interpretation—a "real undercover agent"—followed by the picture. It is impossible to tell what the order is, since the whole is lost within two other levels of interpretation: the narrator's interpretations of the ad and of the responses of the "hipless eleven-year-olds."

Both items are further complicated by the problem of time, the latter even more obviously so than the former. It at first seemed that the sequence: picture, interpretation, facts, was chronological. But this is confused when the question of the informing sign(s) is raised. In the ad we can have no certainty, even from the beginning, because the ad appears a whole in a way the sequence of the first item couldn't approximate. Picture, interpretation, and facts come all at the same time until translated, signified, by an interpreter.

Understanding, according to the narrator, takes place in synchronic time, where events are seen arranged like the signs in the ad. Thrown "backward in space and time, I am beginning to understand how I went wrong, how we all go wrong" (*CBDC*, 108). Understanding is seeing the past from the perspective of the future, the future from the perspective of the past. Yet understanding implies positive knowledge and, as we read earlier, the narrator discovers the emptiness of signs, the tools of, and for, such positive knowledge. Understanding implies distinction: true from false, good from evil, past from future, callowness from maturity. But, immersed in synchrony, such distinctions break down; or, rather, they change form. "The distinction between children and adults, while probably useful for some purposes, is at bottom a specious one, I feel. There are only individual egos, crazy for love" (*CBDC*, 108).

With all his new-found wisdom, the narrator behaves in such a way that his eleven-year-old contemporaries, like the adults in his other life, judge him to be naive (*CBDC*, 111). Thus, though this perspective seems to promise understanding, it shows that there is only nothing to understand, that a true synchronic display is impossible because every sign, itself a repetition and capable only of repetition, stretches backwards and forwards into infinity.

In his "Dedicatoria y Prólogo" to "Seven Exemplary Fictions" Robert Coover expresses a determination to follow in the footsteps of Cervantes in struggling "against the unconscious mythic residue in human life . . . against adolescent thought-modes and exhausted art forms."[17] The structuralist, however, might find Coover to be immersed in the very myth of Logos from which he takes pains to extricate himself. His statements indicate a belief in such informing Ideas as "Being," "Beauty," "Design," and the "Poetic Imagination."[18] Fortunately or unfortunately, his language is not entirely amenable to his purposes for it; it forever carries with it that "mythic residue" like a Siamese twin. In fact Coover's language tends to critique such purposes while it is in the act of attempting to realize them. Beneath the fairly obvious struggle against outmoded forms is a deeper, if imperfectly realized, struggle intrinsic not just to Coover's language but to language in general. Coover's case is particularly interesting, however, because of the apparent opposition between his recognition of this struggle in his fiction and his failure to, or determination not to, recognize it in his extra-fictional comments.

This opposition makes itself felt in a number of ways in THE UNIVERSAL BASEBALL ASSOCIATION, INC., J. HENRY WAUGH, PROP. The title character has invented a game (or rather a whole cosmos, since it grows to include not only baseball but also politics, mathematics, religion, philosophy, music, and so on) which is gradually absorbing more and more of the real world in which he lives as a bachelor accountant. A number of fortunate throws of his dice enable a young pitcher to throw a perfect game. But Henry's joy at this event is soon succeeded by anguish when the hero, Damon Rutherford, is killed by a pitched ball thrown by Jock Casey. Henry's world stops and so does that of the UBA. He tries to free himself from his Association but rationalizes that he should stay in at least to "complete the season." He tries to bring a friend into the game, a move that proves disastrous even before Lou spills beer all over the charts and records. For the first time Henry decides to interfere with his system, to alter the fall of the dice so that Casey will himself be killed by a line drive off the bat of Royce Ingram, Damon's former batting mate. Henry's system responds to its violation with a vengeance, causing him to vomit "a red and golden rainbow arc of half-curded pizza" over his Association.[19]

Finally Henry is fired from his job for missing work, and soon he apparently succeeds in totally merging the real world with the world of his game. The last chapter takes place several Association-years afterwards. It concerns the preparation for a game participated in by many of the ancestors of those playing in the Rutherford-Casey-Ingram years, a game which ritualistically reenacts the pivotal event—the killing of Damon—that has become the mythic cornerstone for the Association's competing philosophies of life.

An apparent transformation of the original opposition between an Ideal and a deconstructed[20] language is realized in the form of Henry's two worlds. At first, both are clearly demarcated, though he is able to move easily between them. Henry creates the world of the Association and this latter world, in turn, informs his perception of the real world. He is conscious of himself as both in and out of the Association; he sets it in motion and yet he is surprised by it. It is the tension, the opposition between the two worlds, which keeps Henry alive, or gives him the "youth" for which he credits his Association (6). Gradually, however, the opposition breaks down and Henry more and more identifies himself with his created world. Correspondingly, he sees the outside world as alien. "Their? mine; it was all the same" (157-58). "He didn't seem to be playing with Lou, but through him, and the way through was dense and hostile" (185).

Because they are both filtered through Henry's signification, a change in one of the worlds produces a change in the other, in effect transforms the other.[21] "Hunched-up cars pushed through the streets like angry defeated ballplayers jockeying through the crowds on their way to the showers" (46). Yet the one world is ostensibly real and the other fictional, a distinction which continues to exist even when it is dissolved at the end of the novel. (The reader, conditioned by the patterns of the book, continues to insert it.) Thus Coover is obviously mirroring the duality in his own relationship with the Association, the life-sustaining tension between, on the one hand, dissolution into the fictional creation and, on the other hand, the obvious manipulation that paradoxically signals his withdrawal from that creation. This tension is the meaning of *the* Association, or of Association, period.[22] It is the meaning of any oppositional relationship, in short, of any relationship, since all associations, linguistic or otherwise, are necessarily oppositional.

The pivotal opposition within the Association itself is "the almost perfect balance between offence and defense." "When he'd finally decided to settle on his own baseball game, Henry had spent the better part of two months just working with the problem of odds and equilibrium points in an effort to approximate that complexity" (20). This opposition finds its most effective statement in the disruptive duel between Damon and Jock Casey. The disruption threatens to be crucial until someone finds a way to rationalize it, submit it to language. (Such harmony is, of course, ironic, since the disruption of the duel is mirrored in the language meant to ameliorate it.)

> It was all there in the volumes of the Book and in the records, but now it needed a new ordering, perspective, personal vision, the disclosure of pattern, because he'd discovered—who had discovered? Barney maybe—yes, Barney Bancroft had discovered that perfection wasn't a thing, a closed moment, a static fact, but *process*, yes, and the process was transformation, and so Casey had participated in the perfection too, maybe more than anybody else, for even Henry had been affected, and Barney was going to write it. . . .
> And what would Bancroft call it? *The Beginnings*, maybe. Or: *The UBA Story. Abe Flint's Legacy. The UBA in the Balance*. "Yes, that's it!" (211-12)

Bancroft's death was a kind of synthesis for the Duel. . . . (224) "Synthesis" doesn't last long in this or any linguistic world, and Bancroft's suicide (concurrent with Henry's?)[23] doesn't "round off" (Henry's term for the function of his own player-obituaries) the process of opposition; it merely extends the transformational process by negating its own content.

Such a deconstruction is apparent even as Henry/Barney evolves the future out of the past and the present. "And so Barney's history of the Association: revealing the gradual evolution toward Guildsman principles, and using the Rutherford-Casey event as the culminating moment, revolving toward the New Day. . . . Of course, Pat Monday might want to carry that history another step, but never mind, for the moment he's no threat. [It turns out that Monday exercises just such a role as is here imagined for him.] . . . "What we want in this Association is participation—not in real time—but in significant time!" (217)

The final chapter is the realization of Henry's injunction to the Association to participate in significant rather than real time. The tension between the two is still there; but it is transformed. For all intents and purposes time stops for Henry when Casey kills Damon and Ingram kills Casey (203). "Significant time" is "the culminating moment," the appearance of the triple ones which killed Damon and, superimposed on this moment, Henry's disruption (ostensibly for the sake of balance) of the pattern in order to kill Casey. The opposition between real and significant time has been transformed into an opposition between Damon and Casey. When the latter is itself formalized —but still subject to repetition or interpretation—by Barney's history, *The UBA in the Balance*, the form of the opposition remains the same, its content merely is changed by being transferred from the plane of the story which imagines Henry (the "frame tale," as it were) to the story which Henry imagines and finally to the plane of the story imagined by Henry's story. Now the opposition between the two times becomes an opposition between the real time of the players in year CLVII of the Association and the "mythic residue," the significant generative time of the duel between the "original" players, a tension between (imagined) freedom and (imagined) pattern (227). Like the oppositions between Henry's life inside and outside the Association and the opposition between Damon and Casey, this one is highly ambiguous. The value to be attributed is forever subject to reinterpretation. In fact, the process of interpretation has replaced the actual occurence as the significant generative event to the point that some "writers even argue that Rutherford and Casey never existed—nothing more than another of the ancient myths of the sun, symbolized as a victim slaughtered by the monster or force of darkness" (223-4).

As the story reaches its conclusion it increasingly convolutes, characters reflect on, as well as reflect—by their names and ritualized actions—their origins and destinations.[24] But they find that they cannot identify either; there is no apparent rationale, no intelligible system of cause and effect to give meaning to their experience. To have one's beginnings and endings lost in infinity, to be unable clearly to demarcate polarities even in one's own existence, is, in a very real sense, to issue from nothing, nothing, that is, but pattern or patterning itself.[25] Words like characters, also begin to reflect each other, not only because of their double meanings, leading outward, but through their rhymes, leading inward.[26] Sounds, like characters and themes, are self-perpetuating, self-transforming; but when they mock themselves they are also self-negating.

In the end Coover reminds us that he, like Henry, can set up the dice. Seriously, or ironically, meaning is offered up as a willed appreciation of the moment, imaginatively transformed; no matter that emptiness surrounds it, no matter that one lives within the dream of a dead man.[27] Unlike Donald Barthelme's character in "The Glass Mountain," Coover is unable to throw the "beautiful enchanted symbol" down the mountain to his "acquaintances." Perhaps he, like his character's character's character . . . would like to believe that the moving baseball (a metaphor for "process") is "alive," that it is the source of life in all the contexts through which it moves; yet he also sees that it only has life when it is illuminated by a "sun," when it is animated by someone throwing or hitting it. And since Coover has hollowed out that sun and those ballplayers, since he has hollowed out the worlds through which that baseball must move, he has effectively shown us that the baseball has no more, and no less, life than its contexts.

Saussure talked of language or any sign-system as functioning like chess. He might just as well have used baseball as a paradigm, not only because of its system of oppositions but because of its players, empty without attributed value. In this sense the UBA records both a series of abstractions from reality and, at the same time, contains all of reality. The ultimately self-defining, self-generating UBA is a network of signs derived from the game of baseball. But the latter is itself a ritual, an interpretation of rules which are, in turn, an interpretation of what should obtain in "life," i.e., balance, cause and effect, "justice," predictability, surprise, and so on. The playing of the game—throwing the dice, keeping the scorecard—derives from and gives life to the abstraction that is the Universal Baseball Association. Setting down the records, maintaining the archives, developing the politics, registering the conversation and the songs, remembering the history, all are further transformations of the "original" sign system or its derivations. Each sign seems to function like a vector of force which divides into two more force vectors (along lines similar to those described by Henry Adams) which themselves divide, and so on, thus accounting for the "shifting and ambiguous" nature of the interplay of signs.

The records of a particular game or of the game itself (history) are an abstraction of the game which effectually dispenses with the actual game. "I found out the scorecards were enough. I didn't need the games" (166). The action of Henry's league represents a transformation of the scorecards from "real" life, while *its* history, as recorded by Barney Bancroft, becomes the basis for the meta-UBA of the last chapter. All of these levels of signification exist not only in a diachronic ("real time") relationship with each other, but also in a synchronic ("significant time") relationship. This we see in the last chapter and in such remarks as: "Damon was not only creating the future, he was doing something to the past, too" (22). Seen diachronically, in Coover's world as in that of Gass and Barthelme, there is change, development, progress or regress, even staticity (which implies the possibility of progress or regress). Seen synchronically, there is perpetual repetition.

NOTES

1. In "The Celebration of Solipsism: A New Trend in American Fiction," *Modern Fiction Studies*, 19 (1973), 5-16, Arlen J. Hansen contends that Gass, Coover, and Barthelme, among others, are representative of a "new solipsism," which attempts to have it both ways. "The challenge to the solipsists, then, is to find a perspective that articulates the value and inescapability of solipsism and yet avoids its delusions. The viability of the new solipsism, as opposed to the old, is that it seeks *creative adjustment* to whatever the mind takes to be 'out there' " (14). Depending on what the last sentence means, such an argument may very well be true; but discussing the meaning of a particular *content* in the context of a claim that the writer is a solipsist reminds one of the necessarily contradictory position of Kierkegaard's "Apostle of Silence."
2. *In the Heart of the Heart of the Country and Other Stories* (New York: Harper & Row, 1969), pp. 7-8. All other references are to this edition.
3. See, for example, Pa's speech damning Pederson, on page 5.
4. This is presented symbolically in Jorge's remembrance of the picture-book episode (p. 67).
5. See his description of the stove at home on page 43 and the train of association engendered by the Pederson stove on pages 78-79.
6. He leaves *after* a section where Jorge interprets the snow with great lyrical intensity and right *before* Jorge remembers himself as the murderer in Eden—see page 67.
7. "The snow came to my thighs, but I was thinking of where the kid lay on the kitchen table in all that dough, pasty with whiskey and water, like spring had come all at once to our kitchen, and our all the time not knowing he was there, had thawed the top of his grave off and left him for us to find . . ." (14). "He was in the wind now and in the cold now and sleepy now just like me. . . .It was good I was glad he was there it wasn't me was there sticking up bare in the wind on a horse like a stick with the horse most likely stopped by this time with his bowed head bent into the storm, and I wouldn't like lying all by myself out there in the cold white dark, dying all alone out there, being buried out there while I was still trying to breathe, knowing I'd only come slowly to the surface in the spring and would soon be soft in the new sun and worried by curious dogs" (72).

8. Gass gives us a paradigm for this on pages 21-2 when he defines the situation of the story-teller through Big Hans. Hans is described by Jorge as one who rubs life into hitherto lifeless words and then has to bear the consequences of what he has done. But the teller's indispensible alter-ego, the listener, is here given the equally ambivalent position of one who denies that life but who, by his denial, affirms the existence of that which he denies.
9. *Unspeakable Practices, Unnatural Acts* (New York: Farrar, Straus & Giroux, 1968), pp. 139, 11. For convenience' sake the following abbreviations will be used: *UPUA* for *Unspeakable Practices, Unnatural Acts; CBDC* for *Come Back Dr. Caligari* (Boston: Little, Brown, 1964); *S* for *Sadness* (New York: Farrar, Straus & Giroux, 1972); *SW* for *Snow White* (New York: Atheneum, 1972).
10. James Dickey, *Sorties* (Garden City, N.Y.: Doubleday, 1971), p. 88. Tony Tanner, *City of Words* (New York: Harper & Row, 1971), p. 406.
11. Paul de Man, *Blindness and Insight: Essays in the Rhetoric of Contemporary Criticism* (New York: Oxford University Press, 1971), p. 108.
12. Cf., the fondness of the avowed and the proto-structuralists for Borges, especially his library of Babel and its book with no, or an infinite, middle.
13. This, however, is itself a potentially self-subversive statement, since fragments are hardly forms in any traditional sense.
14. Yet development, like form, is redefined by Barthelme's context.
15. At the "heart" of any linguistic structure, according to Jacques Derrida, is not the rule of the game but "freeplay," the (action of) game itself. "Structure, Sign and Play in the Discourse of the Human Sciences," in Richard Macksey and Eugenio Donato, eds., *The Languages of Criticism and the Sciences of Man* (Baltimore: Johns Hopkins, 1970), pp. 264-67, *et passim.*
16. Hence they are coherent, and therefore "valid," a term which Roland Barthes (as quoted in the "Introduction" to *Structuralism*, Michael Lane, ed. [London: Jonathan Cape, 1970] pp. 36-7) feels is a more relevant one than "true" in its application to language.
17. *Pricksongs and Descants* (New York: New American Library, 1969), p. 77.
18. Ibid., pp. 78-9.
19. THE UNIVERSAL BASEBALL ASSOCIATION, INC., J. HENRY WAUGH, PROP. (New York: New American Library, 1968), p. 208. All references are to this edition.
20. Such a language, many structuralists say is the only *real* language.
21. Extending the concept Barthes presents in his discussion of the "commutation test" (*Elements of Semiology* [Boston: Beacon, 1967], pp. 65-67), one could say that this effectually proves their reciprocal relationship as signified and signifier.
22. Insofar as the ideal world corresponds to the signified and the real world to the signifier, the "meaning" is, of course, in the association of the two, the *action* of signification.
23. Henry is not mentioned in the last chapter. He is no longer self-conscious, which for him means that he no longer lives in both worlds. Whether he has ceased to live in the world of Lou and Zifferblat physically as well as mentally is irrelevant. What is relevant is that the game's structure has taken over; it has a life of its own; it is capable of writing itself.
24. "Or maybe it just happened. . . . Another accident in a chain of accidents: worse even than invention. Invention, even by a Monday or a Trench, implies a need and need implies purpose; accident implies nothing, nothing at all, and nothing is the one thing that scares Hardy Ingram"

(224-25). "We have no mothers, Gringo. The ripening of their wombs is nothing more than a ceremonious parable. We are mere ideas, hatched whole and hapless, here to enact old rituals of resistance and rot" (230). "Beyond each game, he sees another, and yet another, in endless and hopeless succession. . . . And when, after being distracted by the excitement of a game, he returns at night to the dread, it is worse than ever, compounded with shame and regret. He wants to quit—but what does he mean, 'quit'? The game? Life? Could you separate them?" (238).

25. "Or is it for the record books that we go on, exposing our destinies? 'Exposing our destinies'—that book Raspberry gave him, called *Equilibrium Through Intransigence*. It was Raspberry Schultz one day who told him: 'I don't know if there's really a record-keeper up there or not, Paunch. But even if there weren't, I think we'd have to play the game as though there were.' Would we? Is that reason enough? Continuance for its own inscrutable sake" (239).

26. Raspberry Schultz, who ponders about the "record-keeper" "up there," is one who (like his creator) is said to have "turned . . . to the folklore of game theory, and plays himself some device with dice" (234). The reflections here, of course, are multiple, both in kind and in number.

27. "And then suddenly Damon sees, *must* see, because astonishingly he says: 'Hey, wait, buddy! you *love* this game don't you?'

. . . .

And the black clouds break up, and dew springs again to the green grass, and the stands hang on, and his own oppressed heart leaps alive to give it one last try.

. . . it's all irrelevant, it doesn't even matter that he's going to die, all that counts is that he is *here* and here's The Man and here's the boys and there's the crowd, the sun, the noise.

'It's not a trial,' says Damon, glove tucked in his armpit, hands working the new ball. . . . 'It's just what it is.' Damon holds the baseball up between them. It is hard and white and alive in the sun.

He laughs. It's beautiful, that ball. He punches Damon lightly in the ribs with his mitt. 'Hang loose,' he says, and pulling down his mask, trots back behind home plate" (242).

BIBLIOGRAPHY

Barthes, Roland. *Writing Degree Zero. Elements of Semiology*, trans. Annette Lavers and Colin Smith. Boston: Beacon, 1970.

———. *Mythologies*, trans. Annette Lavers. New York: Hill & Wang, 1972.

de Man, Paul. *Blindness and Insight: Essays in the Rhetoric of Contemporary Criticism*. New York: Oxford University Press, 1971.

———. "Semiology and Rhetoric." *Diacritics*, 3 (Fall, 1973), 27-33.

Derrida, Jacques. "Positions." *Diacritics*, 2 (Winter, 1972), 35-43.

———. "Positions." *Diacritics*, 3 (Spring, 1973), 33-46.

Donato, Eugenio and Richard Macksey, eds. *The Languages of Criticism and the Sciences of Man: The Structuralist Controversy*. Baltimore: Johns Hopkins, 1970.

Ehrmann, Jacques, ed. *Structuralism. Yale French Studies*, 36-37 (1966).

Foucault, Michel. *Madness and Civilization*, trans. Richard Howard. New York: Mentor, 1965.

Funt, David. "Piaget and Structuralism." *Diacritics*, 1 (Fall, 1973), 15-20.

Girard, René. *Deceit, Desire, and the Novel: Self and Other in Literary Structure*, trans. Yvonne Freccero. Baltimore: Johns Hopkins, 1965.

———. "Levi-Strauss, Frye, Derrida and Shakespearean Criticism." *Diacritics* 3 (Fall, 1973), 34-37.

Jameson, Fredric. *The Prison-House of Language: A Critical Account of Structuralism and Russian Formalism*. Princeton: Princeton University Press, 1972.

Lane, Michael, ed. *Structuralism*. London: Jonathan Cape, 1970.

Macksey, Richard, ed. *Velocities of Change: Critical Essays from MLN*. Baltimore: Johns Hopkins, 1974.

Miller, J. Hillis. "*Natural Supernaturalism.*" *Diacritics*, 2 (Winter 1972), 6-13.

———. "Williams' *Spring and All* and the Progress of Poetry." *Daedalus* (Spring, 1970), 405-434.

Simon, John K., ed. *Modern French Criticism: From Proust and Valery to Structuralism*. Chicago: University of Chicago Press, 1972.